# KANGAROOS

## BIOLOGY OF THE LARGEST MARSUPIALS

### Terence J. Dawson

*Illustrated by*
**ANNE MUSSER** *and* **JILLIAN HALLAM**

**COMSTOCK PUBLISHING ASSOCIATES** a division of
**CORNELL UNIVERSITY PRESS** | Ithaca, New York

To my parents,
Jack and Rose Dawson,
who loved the open plains of western New South Wales.

And to Geoff Sharman and John Calaby
whose insights and advice got me started
on my researches into kangaroo biology.

First published 1995 by Cornell University Press.

Library of Congress Cataloging-in-Publication data

Dawson, Terence J.
  Kangaroos: biology of the largest marsupials/Terence J. Dawson.
    p.  cm.
  Includes bibliographical references (p.  ) and index.
  ISBN 0-8014-8262-3
  1. Kangaroos. I. Title
QL737.M35D39 1995
599.2—dc20                                                                94-33542

Printed in Australia by Southwood Press Pty Ltd

# CONTENTS

# PREFACE

My father was a railwayman and the family was moved around country New South Wales. As a consequence, I grew up wandering the bush around towns like Nyngan in the State's central west and Albury on the Murray River. Seeing kangaroos was always special for me and, because of my curiosity about them, Ellis Troughton's *Furred Animals of Australia* came as a Christmas present when I was twelve. My scientific interest in kangaroos, however, had its origins in the United States. I was a postdoctoral fellow in Knut Schmidt-Nielsen's comparative physiology group at Duke University, North Carolina, and I was often asked about kangaroos. Americans assumed that an Australian would know all about them. I didn't, and my curiosity was rekindled.

The 1960s were a time when you could fall on your feet. I got a lectureship in zoology at the University of New South Wales, where Geoff Sharman was setting up a kangaroo research group. The University had also recently acquired Fowlers Gap Station and was developing it as an arid zone research station. To live in Sydney as well: what more could a New South Welshman ask for?

At that time there was a burst of interest in kangaroos, partly driven by conflict between conservation and pastoral interests. The initial focus was at the CSIRO Division of Wildlife, but it spread out to the universities and

State organisations. As a result, an integrated understanding of the biology of kangaroos is now emerging. The biology of the large kangaroos is more complex and interesting than I could possibly have imagined when I first watched them in the bush around Nyngan.

I thank many colleagues and students for their input into my work with kangaroos. In my early days at the University of New South Wales and Fowlers Gap Research Station, Eleanor Russell and Leon Hughes were fine colleagues; we learnt a lot together with Geoff and it was mostly fun. David Croft has been a great Fowlers Gap stalwart and I have relied much on his group's studies of behavioural ecology. Thanks are due too to my many good students for their contributions. Two of these people particularly come to mind when I think about kangaroos — Martin Denny, my first 'kangaroo' PhD, and Glen Edwards, one of my most recent. Their efforts and dedication went far beyond what was necessary. For her skill at diet analysis and her cheerful field assistance Beverley Ellis is specially acknowledged.

Those who have helped with the production of this book must be thanked for their forbearance. There was always something else that I needed to do more urgently. Julia Collingwood and Rex Parry of the University of New South Wales Press have been very supportive of the whole Natural History Series and of *Kangaroos* in particular. Dr Jill Hallam's diagrams and Anne Musser's drawings have added much to the text.

Without my wife Lyndall's help, both scientific and editorial, this book would never have seen the light of day. She provided many ideas and removed much scientific jargon during her continual editing. I especially thank her for her forbearance.

## CHAPTER 1

# WHAT ARE KANGAROOS?

## INTRODUCTION

Kangaroos are among the strangest of all mammals. This is not because they are marsupials and keep their young in a pouch, but because they *hop*. Many types of marsupial are spread throughout Australia and Central/South America and, apart from their unusual method of reproduction, they are really not much different from other mammals. However, hopping is very uncommon among vertebrates; otherwise being used only by frogs and some small desert mammals. Apart from kangaroos and their relatives, no vertebrates larger than about 5 kg hop. There is no evidence in fossil history of other large hopping animals.

Kangaroos and their hopping intrigued the earliest European visitors to Australia (Fig. 1.1). Sir Joseph Banks wrote in the journal of his voyage with Captain James Cook on the *Endeavour* from 1768 to 1771:

> Quadripeds we saw but few, and were able to catch few of them that we did see. The largest was called by the natives kangaroo. It is different from any European and indeed any animal I have heard or read of except the Gerbua of Eygpt, which is not larger than a rat when this is as large as a middling Lamb; the largest we shot weighed 84 lb. It may however be easily known

from all other mammals by the singular property of running or rather hopping upon only its hinder legs carrying its fore bent close to its breast; in this manner however it hops so fast that in the rocky bad ground where it is commonly found it easily beat my grey hound, who tho he was fairly started at several killed only one, and that quite a young one.

The name kangaroo was one of the first Aboriginal words introduced into English. It came from the natives at Endeavour River (modern Cooktown) in the far north of Queensland. Cook's party sighted and obtained their first kangaroos there when they put in to repair the *Endeavour* after it was almost wrecked on the Great Barrier Reef.

Kangaroos are the largest living marsupials. They belong to the Superfamily Macropodoidea, the 'big foots' (Fig. 1.2). There are some 62 living species of macropodoids in Australia and New Guinea, ranging from rat-sized species weighing less than one kilogram to species in which the males may weigh up to 90 kg. The largest Family within this group is Macropodinae, the kangaroos and wallabies. Early scientists defined the kangaroos as those species having a hind foot more than 250 mm long. This definition encompassed the six largest species, but overlap between small female kangaroos and some large male wallabies prevents size alone

*Figure 1.1*
*A reproduction of an early poster featuring a 'Kanguroo from Botany Bay'. Londoners are informed of the amazing features of this unique animal from the new colony in the South Seas. The depiction of the kangaroo was based on a painting by George Stubbs done (from skins) in 1771 or 1772.*

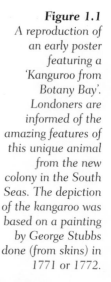

THE WONDERFUL

# KANGUROO
FROM
# BOTANY BAY

THIS amazing, beautiful, and tame Animal, is about five Feet in Height, of a Fawn colour, and diftinguifhes itfelf in Shape, Make, and true Symmetry of Parts, different from all other QUADRUPEDS. Its Swiftnefs, when purfued, is fuperior to the Greyhound: to enumerate its extraordinary Qualities would far exceed the common Limits of a Public Notice. Let it fuffice to obferve, that the Public in general are pleafed, and beftow their Plaudits; the Ingenious are delighted; the Virtuofo and Connoiffeur, are taught to admire! impreffing the Beholder with Wonder and Aftonifhment, at the Sight of this unparalleled Animal from the Southern Hemifphere, that almoft furpaffes Belief; therefore Ocular Demonftration will exceed all that words can defcribe, or Pencil delineate ... Admittance ONE SHILLING each.

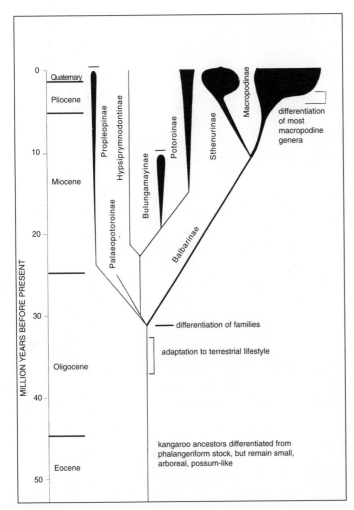

MILLION YEARS BEFORE PRESENT

0

Quaternary

Pliocene

Propleopinae

Hypsiprymnodontinae

Palaeopotoroinae

Bulungamayinae

Potoroinae

Balbarinae

Sthenurinae

Macropodinae

differentiation
of most
macropodine
genera

10

Miocene

20

differentiation of families

adaptation to terrestrial lifestyle

30

Oligocene

40

kangaroo ancestors differentiated from
phalangeriform stock, but remain small,
arboreal, possum-like

Eocene

50

**Figure 1.2**
*Evolution of the
Superfamily
Macropodoidea —
the hopping
marsupials.
The Family
Macropodinae, the
kangaroos and their
kin, represents an
extensive but recent
radiation. After
Flannery (1989).*

from being a reliable characteristic by which to define the group. Nevertheless, by general acceptance the six largest species are now called kangaroos and the smaller species are known as wallabies.

Several characteristics, as well as their size, tend to unite these six species as a group. Of prime importance is the fact that they are grazers — that is, they eat grass as the main component of their diet. Grass can supply much energy, but is not easily digested. The evolution of the anatomical and physiological specialisations that permit this lifestyle is complex and has not occurred often among mammals. Parallel adaptations are found only among ruminants, such as sheep, cattle, antelope and deer. These species, and the kangaroos, have specialised teeth for cropping grass and complex forestomachs for the fermentative breakdown of plant fibre (see Chapter 7).

The six living species of kangaroo fall into four groups: the two grey kangaroos, the red kangaroo, the antilopine kangaroo and the wallaroo–euro group. None of these species is endangered, unlike many of their smaller relatives such as bettongs, hare-wallabies and some wallabies. Between them the kangaroos range over most of Australia. In some areas only one species may be found but in other places several occur. Such is the case at my study area at Fowlers Gap Arid Zone Research Station in western New South Wales (Plate 1). Here four species are found, these being red kangaroos, euros, eastern grey kangaroos and western grey kangaroos. Although they all occur on this 40,000 hectare station, there are obvious differences in the preferred living areas of each species. The differences can be related to the species' habitat preferences right across the continent. This book describes significant recent studies of the biology of kangaroos in a variety of locations throughout Australia (Fig. 1.3).

# FOSSIL HISTORY AND EVOLUTION OF KANGAROOS

The first appearance of the large grazing kangaroos in Australia and the path of their evolution have been somewhat of a mystery. The fossil record was poorly known until recently. Now good fossil discoveries, especially those made by Mike Archer's University of New South Wales group at Riversleigh in north-west Queensland, are providing clues and some answers. The place of the large kangaroos in the evolutionary history of the Macropodoidea is suggested in Fig. 1.2.

The earliest ancestors of kangaroos probably derived from small, tree-dwelling possum-like marsupials about 50 million years before the present (MYBP). Around 30 MYBP some of these pre-kangaroos came down out of the trees of the rainforests that then covered most of Australia and the real history of the kangaroos and hopping began. The structural changes that accompanied this shift to the ground are not understood yet, but it seems that it was the acquisition of hopping that led to the success of these new-comers to the forest floor.

By about 25 MYBP the evolution of macropodoids was well under way and swift small rat-kangaroos darted through the forest undergrowth. The Miocene-aged Riversleigh fossils show at least four distinct families derived from these rat-kangaroos: the hypsiprymnodontines, the potoroines, the balungamayines and the propleopines. The hypsiprymnodontines are suggested to be the most primitive. The five-toed musky rat-kangaroo of the rainforests of north Queensland is a descendant of this group. The potoroines survive today as the potoroos and bettongs. They have had a long history but are now endangered by the activities of humans. The balunga-mayines are an extinct group that underwent considerable speciation in the Miocene, 10–20 million years ago. Their tooth morphology had similarities with the modern macropodine kangaroos. The pro-pleopines (which included very unkangaroo-like carnivorous forms) are also now extinct.

*Figure 1.3*
*Map of Australia showing the sites of some major studies of the biology of kangaroos.*

*Key:*
*AS, Alice Springs;*
*BH, Bakers Hill;*
*B, Bago Forest;*
*FG, Fowlers Gap;*
*K, Kinchega;*
*KI, Kangaroo Island;*
*M, Mardi Station;*
*TC, Tero Creek;*
*T, Tibooburra;*
*WC, Wallaby Creek;*
*W, Wiluna.*

*Also shown is the 250 mm rainfall isohyet.*

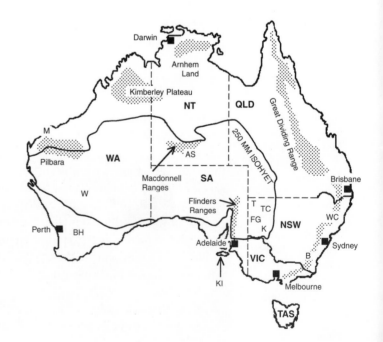

The last late Pleistocene survivor of this line, *Propleopus oscillans*, stood about two metres tall.

The true kangaroos, as we know them now, arrived late in the evolutionary history of Australia. The fossil family of balbarine kangaroos, which probably gave rise to the macropodines (the present wallabies and kangaroos), is represented in the early Riversleigh fossil deposits by rat-sized animals. Even at that time their teeth showed adaptations for a herbivorous diet, which suggests the development of a complex stomach, a feature crucial to the later success of kangaroos. The extensive radiations of the kangaroos and their relatives accompanied the drying out of Australia and the spread of grasslands. This process was well under way by 4–5 million years ago, in the Pliocene period, when the first species clearly related to the modern grey kangaroos and wallaroos begin to appear in the fossil record. The red kangaroo is the most recently evolved kangaroo. Its fossil record does not go back beyond the Pleistocene period, 1–2 million years ago, and its evolution appears to coincide with the spread of aridity and deserts in Australia. A close relationship between the red kangaroo and the wallaroos and euros has been suggested, but as yet no fossil evidence is known to indicate the precise ancestry of the red kangaroo.

## THE SIGNIFICANCE OF HOPPING

The amazing and unique feature of kangaroos and wallabies is their mode of locomotion (Fig. 1.4, Plate 4). No other large animals have used hopping as an evolutionary adaptation, which indicates that there is something very special about kangaroos. The body shape, especially of the hindquarters and tail, is highly specialised. This is seen clearly from the skeleton (Fig. 1.5). This leads us to ask whether the underlying principle of locomotion in kangaroos has similarities in other fast mammals. Also, if hopping is so special, what are its advantages?

To help answer these questions, the energy cost of hopping has been measured in laboratory studies and compared with the energy costs of

*Figure 1.4*
*Kangaroos are obviously specialised for hopping. The greatly developed hindlimbs and tail are contrasted with the much reduced forelegs.*

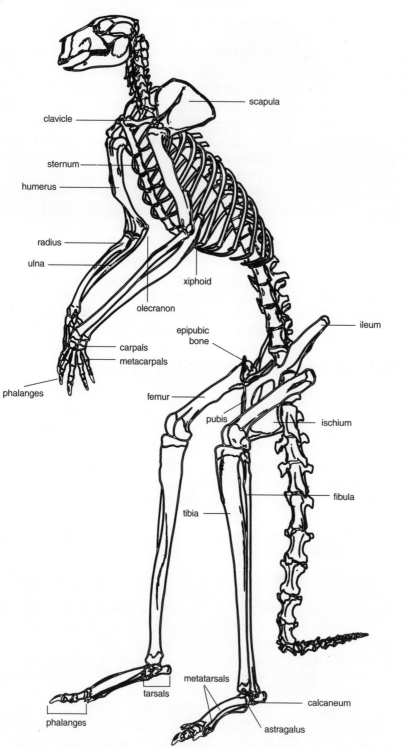

**Figure 1.5**
*The skeleton of a red kangaroo showing the extreme specialisation for hopping in the hind limbs, lower back and tail.*

scapula

clavicle

sternum

humerus

radius

ulna

xiphoid

olecranon

carpals

metacarpals

phalanges

epipubic bone

femur

pubis

ileum

ischium

fibula

tibia

metatarsals

tarsals

phalanges

calcaneum

astragalus

*Figure 1.6*

*A red kangaroo walking on a motor-driven treadmill. The lightweight face mask is for the measurement of oxygen use, from which the energy costs of locomotion can be determined. (Photo C. R. Taylor.)*

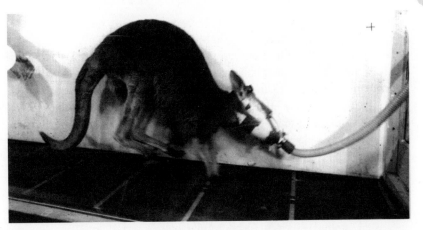

normal running in four-legged animals. Over 25 years ago Richard Taylor and co-workers at Duke and Harvard Universities were studying the energetics of normal walking and running, and in 1973 I took red kangaroos to Harvard University where experiments showed that the kangaroos really differed in their pattern of energy use from that seen in mammals that run. The kangaroos were trained to hop on a treadmill which could move at a range of speeds. The kangaroos were also trained to wear a mask while they hopped so that their oxygen use could be measured (Fig. 1.6). Oxygen use indicates how much metabolic fuel is being burnt and hence the energy cost of locomotion.

In placental mammals that run there is a relatively constant increase in the cost, or power requirement, as speed increases (Fig. 1.7). Quadrupedal marsupials, such as the Tasmanian devil, also follow this pattern but kangaroos do not. During hopping the change in energy cost with changing speed follows an unusual pattern. Kangaroos 'walk' at slow speeds and start to hop as speed increases. When hopping starts its costs are high. However, over a wide range of speeds the energy costs then change little, so a kangaroo travelling at moderate speeds (above about 15 km/h) does so more economically than a running animal of similar size.

This pattern of energy expenditure is explained by the storage of energy in elastic tissues. Energy can be stored for re-use in elastic fibrous tissues, such as tendons, in the same manner as energy is stored in the spring of a pogo stick or in the rubber of a bouncing ball. Studies of the elastic storage of energy during fast locomotion in mammals have been made by McNeil Alexander and colleagues in England. Many parts of the body are involved: tendons, muscles and the vertebral column. The tendonous structures of the limbs, lower back and tail seem to be the greatest contributors to the very high level of energy conservation in hopping kangaroos.

Measurements on treadmills were not practical at speeds above 22–24 km/h, but what happens at higher speeds can be inferred from field

observation. Most animals (for example horses) normally travel at their most comfortable
or economical speed for their various gaits.
For hopping red kangaroos the most comfortable speed is about 20–25 km/h. Energy costs
probably increase above this speed because
the elastic storage of energy cannot increase
indefinitely. Hopping rate or stride frequency
remains constant up to about 40 km/h, with
increases in speed being achieved by increasing only the length of the hop (Fig. 1.7).

If pressed, a red kangaroo can maintain
speeds of around 40 km/h for a couple of
kilometres. Red kangaroos can increase their
speed above 40–45 km/h, but do so only in
emergencies. Then, high-speed bursts usually last for only a few hundred metres. I have
measured speeds up to about 50 km/h in the
wild and speeds of 65–70 km/h have been
reported. At these higher speeds there is a noticeable increase in hop
frequency as well as hop length. The increase in hop frequency appears be
accompanied by a considerable increase in energy use, but exactly how the
energy cost of hopping at maximum speeds is related to the cost of high-
speed running is unknown.

Rodger Kram and Richard Taylor of Harvard University have suggested
that the energy cost of running is related to the time of foot contact with
the ground. The shorter the contact time, as speed increases, the higher the
energy cost. The hypothesis is based on the idea that it is the cost of gen-
erating force in the muscles that determines the overall energy cost. As a
quadruped runs faster it must use additional, quicker responding, muscle
fibres because the time of foot contact becomes much shorter.

Over a wide range of speeds energy use by hopping kangaroos is independent of speed, but the time of their foot contact also decreases with
increasing speeds. This does not fit with the picture just described for
quadrupeds. Rodger Kram spent time with me at Fowlers Gap Research
Station examining this inconsistency. Hopping in red kangaroos was studied in detail using high-speed photography, which can be slowed down for
analysis. As yet, the unique mechanism needed to explain this relationship
between speed and energy use in kangaroos has not been uncovered.

If hopping is so energetically economical why in big animals is it only
found in kangaroos and their relatives? There are two possibilities. A unique
evolutionary adaptation to allow hopping may have occurred early in the history of the Macropodoidea, with the group markedly exploiting this; however,

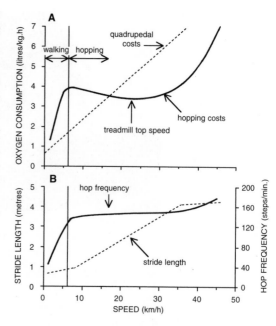

**Figure 1.7**
*(A) Influence of
speed on the energy
costs of hopping in
red kangaroos and
running in
quadrupedal
mammals of a
similar size. Below
about 6 km/h
kangaroos walk
using their tail as a
'fifth' leg. Note the
very irregular pat-
tern for kangaroos.
(B) Change in the
stride length and
hop frequency with
increasing speed in
red kangaroos.
Once hopping
starts, increases in
speed are largely
accomplished by
increasing stride
length. Based on
Dawson and Taylor
(1973).*

we do not yet understand the nature of any such adaptation. Another possibility is that hopping in kangaroos is an unusual form of 'normal' locomotion; but our recent work makes this unlikely. A recently discovered feature of marsupials may prove to be enlightening. Marsupials have a high aerobic capacity for sustained energy use. Sprinting placental mammals, such as the cheetah, use energy stored in their muscles for rapid dashes after prey. Such energy 'storage' may not be as necessary in marsupials. The very high aerobic capacity of the marsupials may mean that kangaroos and wallabies have the 'horsepower' needed to maintain fast hopping for a long time and to go faster than placentals during sustained locomotion. Perhaps it was a combination of this high aerobic capacity of marsupials and some special morphological adaptation that made the macropodoids so successful.

The hopping of kangaroos is not advantageous in all situations. A feature of hopping is that its energetic characteristics change considerably as the size of animals changes. As hopping mammals get bigger they diverge more from a normal quadrupedal pattern, both in body shape and energetics. Small hopping animals, such as potoroos, use quadrupedal locomotion at low speeds and then their locomotion costs are not very different from those of other quadrupeds. Big kangaroos have large benefits at higher speeds but there are problems at low speeds.

At speeds below 6 km/h kangaroos do not hop. They move in a rather odd way, using their heavy tail as an additional support. This slow walking we called 'pentapedal walking' because the tail acts as a fifth leg to help the small forelegs support the kangaroo as the large hind legs are moved forward together. (Contrary to a widespread belief, kangaroos can move their hind legs independently. They are good swimmers and, as they swim, they 'dog paddle' and their hind legs alternate.) The slow walking gait is clumsy and energetically costly. The reason kangaroos resort to this odd mode of locomotion at low speeds is partly related to the gross anatomical specialisation of their hind limbs and the reduction in size of their forelimbs. A physical analysis of the costs of doing work against gravity also indicates it would be even more costly to hop at these low speeds.

The skeletons of a range of giant sthenurines and macropodines which became extinct toward the end of the Pleistocene period suggest an interesting story relating to mobility. The teeth of these extinct forms indicate that they were browsers, not grazers. Browsing, the eating of trees and shrubs, requires a larger than usual stomach to allow for the longer time of digestion of this fibrous food. This means more of a load to carry around, and the browsing species were notable for their stouter proportions. They may well have been slower and less manoeuvrable, and thus easier prey for early Aboriginal men, than the slender grazing kangaroos that we see today. Indeed, the extinction of these giant browsing animals appears to have coincided with the coming of Aboriginal people to Australia (Chapter 9).

# TYPES OF KANGAROO

## GREY KANGAROOS

There are two species of grey kangaroo, the eastern grey, *Macropus giganteus* and the western grey, *Macropus fuliginosus*; these species are closely related but do not interbreed. Between them they inhabit the forests and woodlands of southern and eastern Australia. In recent times they appear to have moved into drier country, probably as a result of the provision of water for domestic stock. Apart from their general grey colour and body shape they are distinguished from the other kangaroos by having the muzzle fully covered by very fine hair; only the margins of the nostrils being ringed with naked black skin (Fig. 2.1). Also, the third upper incisors of the grey kangaroos are markedly larger than in other kangaroos (Fig. 2.1) and this allows the identification of skulls found in the bush. The ranges of eastern and western grey kangaroos overlap in semi-arid areas of New South Wales and south-western Queensland (Fig. 2.2) and correct field identification is not always easy. Colour is the main indicator; the eastern grey kangaroo is more grey while the western species is a dusty brown. The western grey kangaroo also tends to be darker around the head and there may be a blackish patch around the elbow.

**Figure 2.1**
*Characteristics of the head and teeth that can help with the identification of kangaroos, or their remains, in the field. (A) The anterior end of the palate with the incisor teeth (seen also in side view) of the eastern grey kangaroo, western grey kangaroo, euro, and red kangaroo. (B) The pattern of skin and fur on the muzzle distinguishes groups of kangaroos: the eastern grey and western grey kangaroos are similar, the euro, other wallaroos and the antilopine kangaroo are similar; the red kangaroo is distinctive.*

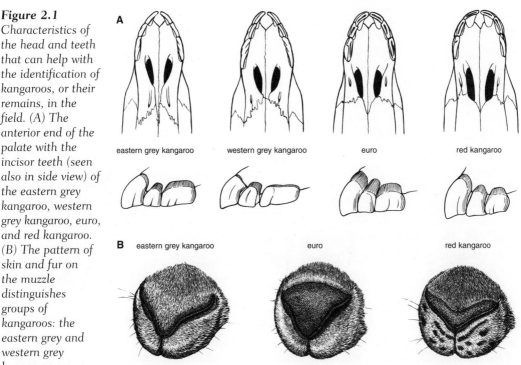

## EASTERN GREY KANGAROO, *MACROPUS GIGANTEUS*

The eastern grey kangaroo is the species which Australians are most likely to have seen in the wild. It is the kangaroo of the wetter areas of eastern Australia, where most Australians live. Yet until recently little accurate information was available about its biology.

*Description* The eastern grey is a large graceful kangaroo with long, soft grey-brown fur (Plates 2 & 12). The belly fur is much lighter and occasionally almost white. Inland animals may be a somewhat darker grey than coastal animals. The paws and the tips of the hind feet and tail tip tend to be darker, at times almost black. In the Tasmanian race the fur is browner and longer and shaggier. There is little difference between the sexes except in size. The males may exceed 70 kg (the largest I have seen was near 90 kg), while the females rarely reach 35 kg.

*Hopping profile* Experienced field workers can identify each species of kangaroo in poor light or at a distance just by the body posture adopted during hopping. Eastern grey kangaroos hop with the back relatively flat and the forelegs low down. The head is held well up, however. When these animals are travelling at speed the tail is noticeably curved upwards and swings up and down more than in other kangaroos.

*Distribution and status* The eastern grey has a broad distribution down the east coast of Australia (Fig. 2.2). It ranges from tropical north Queensland (around Cooktown where it was first collected by Captain Cook at Endeavour River) to southern Victoria and the island state of Tasmania. Eastern grey kangaroos are almost continuously distributed from the east coast and Great Dividing Range westward to the inland plains of eastern Australia. Their habitat is forest and woodland, which changes to low mallee scrub in the far west of their range. These habitats are reflected in local common names for the species, such as 'forester' and 'scrubber'. During the middle of the day they rest in the shelter of trees or scrub and later feed in the clearings. They may also move into more open country to feed and may then be seen in large mobs. Densities of eastern grey kangaroos can peak near 100 per square kilometre (km²) in prime habitat of open grassy woodland in the highlands of eastern Australia.

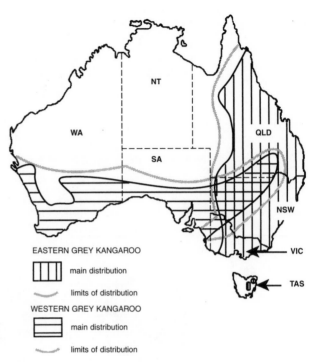

EASTERN GREY KANGAROO

▥ main distribution

〰 limits of distribution

WESTERN GREY KANGAROO

▤ main distribution

〰 limits of distribution

The main populations are restricted to country with more than 250 mm of rain per year, but in relatively recent times they have penetrated further inland along ephemeral creeks lined with river red gums. This extension of range is probably due to the increasing provision of water for sheep and cattle. At Fowlers Gap Research Station in the far west of New South Wales, the eastern grey kangaroo was first seen during very wet years in the mid 1970s. The western grey kangaroo also first appeared on the Station at that time.

Between 1970 and 1990 there was much debate about the status and population size of eastern grey kangaroos. This was initiated by conservation and animal welfare groups who were concerned that the eastern grey (along with other species) was declining in numbers and might eventually become endangered. The debate centred on the impact of harvesting of kangaroos for meat and hides by professional shooters. The discussion initially raged without accurate information. Pressure on governments to ban the export of kangaroo products led to a demand for better population estimates. The only feasible way to get such information over the vast range was aerial counting. Techniques using small low-flying planes were developed and extensive monitoring of kangaroo populations began.

**Figure 2.2**
*Distribution of eastern and western grey kangaroos throughout Australia. The western grey has a largely southern range — suggestions have been made that it be called the southern grey kangaroo. The main population areas are shown and the approximate limits of distributions are indicated. After Caughley (1987).*

Estimates for eastern grey kangaroos on the mainland in 1981 gave a population of about 5 million. This estimate largely covered the population concentrations on the western slopes and plains of Queensland and New South Wales. Much woodland and forest habitat, particularly along the Great Dividing Range, is unsuitable for aerial survey and consequently this number was regarded as being a considerable underestimate. Recent examination of aerial survey techniques, done by checking them against accurate, small-scale ground counts or against detailed helicopter counts, has shown that the sightability of kangaroos from small planes is much lower than originally accepted. Scientists working in this field now consider that the numbers of eastern grey kangaroo are really at least double the 1981 figures. This means that the eastern grey population on the mainland is at least of the order of 10 million. The population in Tasmania, though, is relatively small and active conservation measures are being taken to secure the future of the species there.

Although the eastern grey population is large, and in places such as northern New South Wales and southern Queensland the species is abundant, there are areas where local populations are limited. These areas are primarily in farming country. Land clearance, subdivision and constant ploughing hardly provide ideal habitat, and forest and woodland refuges are few. When animals come out of the few timbered areas to feed they are often killed, usually illegally. They are killed by farmers because of fear of competition with domestic stock, or simply because the ethos among some youths in rural districts is 'if it moves shoot it'. But these attitudes are changing fast and shooting for 'sport' is less common than it was a few years ago.

## WESTERN GREY KANGAROO, *MACROPUS FULIGINOSUS*

There has been uncertainty about the characteristics and distribution of this second species of grey kangaroo. At times western greys have been considered to belong to several distinct species, and at other times they have been treated as subspecies of the eastern grey kangaroo. The matter was clarified by a CSIRO (Commonwealth Scientific and Industrial Research Organisation) group led by Bill Poole in the late 1960s and early 1970s on the basis of biochemical and serological characteristics. The western grey kangaroo, *Macropus fuliginosus*, is now known to be a single species (Plates 3 & 11). It is found in a broad band across southern Australia. The western grey has a range of local common names: black-faced kangaroo, mallee kangaroo, sooty kangaroo and *stinker*, the latter name referring to the strong curry-like smell of the large males.

*Description* There is much variation in this large grey-brown kangaroo. Regional variations are considered to represent distinct subspecies. The most distinctive form is that inhabiting Kangaroo Island, off the coast of South

Australia. Indeed, the first western grey to be scientifically described came from Kangaroo Island. It was collected in 1803 by French naturalists aboard the research vessel *Geographe*. This subspecies, M. *fuliginosus fuliginosus*, is the original type of the species and is very dark sooty brown on the back. It is also distinguished from the other forms by its shorter limbs, ears and tail. Recent work has shown, however, that two supposed mainland subspecies, M. *fuliginosus ocydromus* from Western Australia and M. *f. melanops* from the eastern part of the range, do not represent discrete populations but are at the ends of a cline (a gradually changing population) across southern Australia. The correct name for all mainland forms is therefore M. *fuliginosus melanops*. In the west the species is more brownish and appears more slender, while animals in South Australia, Victoria and New South Wales are stockier in build, dark brown on the head and back, with bluish grey underneath.

*Hopping profile* The hopping profile is similar to that of the eastern grey kangaroo and only when observed side by side with the eastern grey are some differences apparent. The head is held a little lower and appears more solid than in the eastern species. At night, when the colour difference is not so apparent, mistakes in identification occur easily.

*Distribution and status* The western grey kangaroo occurs from near Shark Bay in Western Australia to western Victoria and up through western New South Wales to south-western Queensland (Fig. 2.2). It is closely associated with the southern winter rainfall belt and there have been suggestions that it be called the 'southern grey kangaroo', but as yet this name has not been accepted. It has a high tolerance to plant toxins, notably fluoroacetate (the poison, 1080), which suggests that the species originated in the south-western part of the continent, where shrubs having naturally high levels of this poison occur.

The population size of the western grey kangaroo is unclear because of the doubt about accuracy of aerial surveys. However, it appears that the western grey has a lower abundance than the eastern grey kangaroo or the red kangaroo. The 1981 population estimate for western grey kangaroos was about 1.7 million animals as compared with about 5 million for eastern grey kangaroos.

The highest densities of the western grey kangaroo occur in the western Riverina district of New South Wales and the western edge of the Nullarbor Plain in Western Australia. There have been suggestions that western grey kangaroos have increased their range markedly in recent times but this is doubtful. It is only since 1970 that the extent of the species in New South Wales and Queensland has been appreciated. Mixed mobs of both species of grey kangaroos may be found, although the two species usually occur separately due to their preference for different habitats or 'niches' within a particular area.

These differences are illustrated on the arid edge of their range in western New South Wales at Fowlers Gap Research Station where western grey kangaroos are more common than eastern grey kangaroos. The eastern greys are largely restricted to tall river red gum habitat along the main creek channels, whereas the western greys are often found in association with groups of low prickly wattle trees in small drainage channels. The species do overlap when feeding in the open, but the western grey kangaroos will move further away from heavy cover to feed. In better watered country in the Grampians National Park in western Victoria, Graeme Coulson of Melbourne University found a similar pattern. There the eastern grey kangaroo occurred mainly in a taller eucalytus woodland with an understorey of grass, bracken or shrubs, while the western grey occurred at its highest densities in heathland and low woodland with an understorey of heath. Western grey kangaroos were rarely seen in the tall woodland most favoured by the eastern grey kangaroos. Again, while both species mostly fed within their respective woodland habitats, they did feed together in cleared open grassland.

The status of the western grey kangaroo appears generally secure, though on a regional level populations may be declining. Populations were certainly higher in the past in some higher rainfall parts of their range, the decline being due to the spread of extensive agriculture. This is particularly the case where land clearing, principally for cereal crops, is still taking place. The wheat belts of Western Australia and South Australia and the mallee woodlands of New South Wales and Victoria are the main areas where this is happening. Within established wheat belt areas western grey kangaroos are dependent on remnant patches of woodland.

# RED KANGAROO, MACROPUS RUFUS

There is only one species of red kangaroo, *Macropus rufus*, despite its wide distribution throughout the arid zone of Australia. This powerful but gracefully built animal is the most striking of the kangaroos. The red kangaroo is the characteristic large native mammal of the dry inland of Australia. Its range includes mulga and mallee scrub, saltbush shrubland and arid grassland and desert. Its preference, though, is for open grassy plains with a few scattered trees to provide shade during hot days and shelter from cold winds in winter.

*Description* The red kangaroo is the most handsome of the kangaroos (Plates 4, 5 & 15). While richly coloured, it is not always red. It is a large species with a marked difference in size between the sexes (Fig. 4.2). Kangaroos grow throughout most of their life, so in some areas of restricted shooting males over 80 kg and occasionally over 90 kg are found. Females may grow to 40 kg but their most common size is 23–30 kg. In both sexes the face is delicately marked by an obvious black and white patch at the side of the muzzle and a broad white stripe from the corner of the mouth toward the ear. The tip of the nose, the rhinarium, is naked and sharply outlined (Fig. 2.1). The skin of the rhinarium is granulated in texture and dusky in colour, not shiny black as in the wallaroo group. The males have a rather large bow-shaped nose.

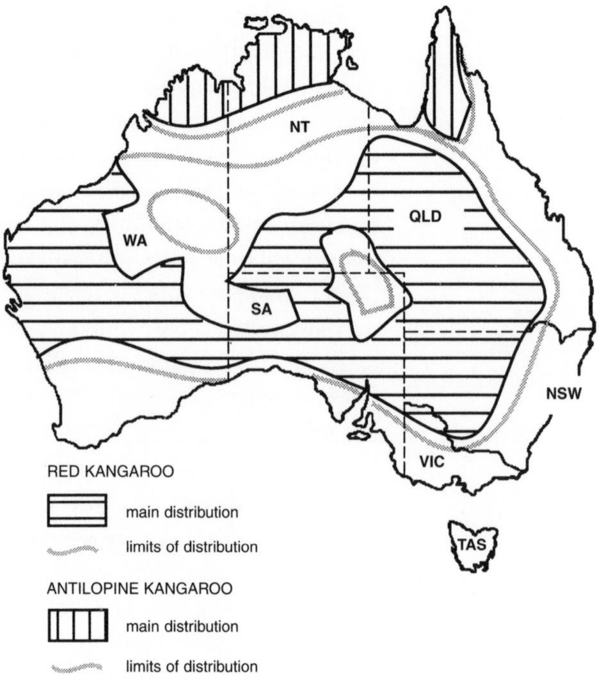

The red kangaroo males are usually red (actually a rich rusty brown) but females are usually a smoky blue and are often called blue-fliers (Plate 5). However, either sex can be either colour or an intermediate shade, and the proportion of animals of each colour can vary from place to place (Fig. 3.7). One survey that I carried out in western New South Wales indicated that of the males 80 per cent were red, 6 per cent blue and 14 per cent an intermediate reddish grey. In the same area the females were 68 per cent smoky blue, 12 per cent red and 20 per cent intermediate shades. Such patterns are seen throughout the range of the red kangaroo in eastern and southern Australia, but in the north-west red is the predominant colour for both sexes (Fig. 3.7). The genetics of this colouring system have not as yet been adequately studied.

The body is not evenly coloured. The under surface is light grey to white, as are the lower parts of the limbs except for the paws and toes which are very dark. The tail tip is also pale and this easily allows separation of the blue-fliers from the grey kangaroos with their dark tail tips.

*Hopping profile* Red kangaroos travel with their backs flat and the head low, in line with the back. The tail is not as curved nor does it swing as much as in the grey kangaroos.

*Distribution and status* Red kangaroos occur over most of the central part of Australia in areas of less than 500 mm annual rainfall. Their highest densities are in the rangelands of western New South Wales where sheep are grazed (Fig. 2.3). This unexpected phenomenon may be due to changes associated with sheep grazing. In this region red kangaroos, along with

RED KANGAROO

main distribution

limits of distribution

ANTILOPINE KANGAROO

main distribution

limits of distribution

**Figure 2.3**
*Distribution of red and antilopine kangaroos throughout Australia. Red kangaroos occur in the arid and semi-arid interior, while the antilopine has its home in the tropical woodlands of the north. After Caughley (1987) and Richardson and Sharman (1976).*

sheep, are protected from dingos by the 'dog fence' along large sections of the border of New South Wales with South Australia and Queensland. Permanent water has been provided for stock throughout this dry country, and on top of this sheep have modified the environment, perhaps to a greater extent than have cattle in other parts of Australia.

Apart from the concentration in western New South Wales the red kangaroo is variably spread throughout arid Australia. The species was once considered to be nomadic, with mobile mobs ranging across the landscape. This is now known to be a myth. Occasional adults and some young red kangaroos do disperse widely, but the overall population is largely sedentary.

In western New South Wales red kangaroos have a preference for open habitats with occasional patches of shade trees such as common mulga (*Acacia aneura*) or prickly wattle (*A. victoriae*). At Mardi Station in the Fortescue River region of Western Australia, where Tony Oliver of the Western Australia Department of Conservation and Land Management has worked extensively, the typical red kangaroo habitat is extensive grass plains with small patches of snakewood (*Acacia xiphophylla*) between creeklines, and shallow drainage channels containing belts of common mulga. Red kangaroos in this region do not utilise large tracts of country containing spinifex (*Triodia*), a very spiny grass.

Red kangaroos are considered to be the most abundant of the kangaroos; the count in 1981 was 8.4 million. Actually, eastern greys may have a larger population, but they are harder to see during aerial surveying. If recent work on the sightability of kangaroos during aerial counting is correct then population estimates for red kangaroos will also have to be substantially increased.

## WALLAROO–EURO GROUP

Wallaroos and the euro are a varied group of closely related kangaroos. Two species are now recognised within the group: *Macropus robustus*, which consists of four accepted subspecies, and *Macropus bernardus*. Wallaroos and the euro may be distinguished from other kangaroos by their stocky shape. Males have very solid shoulders and forearms and both sexes have shorter limbs than other kangaroos do, especially the hind legs. This is an adaptation for supporting a heavy body while leaping among the rocks of their habitat. The shorter, broad hind feet have roughened soles to give good traction on the rocks. Males rarely weigh more than 50 kg; females are less than half this size. The nose is entirely naked and black between the nostrils. The incisor teeth are also distinctive (Fig. 2.1).

Wallaroos and euros hop with a more upright posture than other kangaroos do. Their backs appear to be at about 45 degrees to the horizontal. The forelegs are held close to the body and they seem to take shorter hops than other species. They may appear less agile than other species in open country but they move easily and with little apparent effort over the roughest hillsides.

## 'ROBUSTUS' SUBSPECIES

In its various subspecific guises *Macropus robustus* is common throughout most of mainland Australia except Victoria and the south of Western Australia. Despite their relative abundance, members of this group are infrequently seen because of their association with mountains and rocky hill country. Because of their close association with such habitats their distribution is discontinuous, resulting in considerable variation and the development of subspecies.

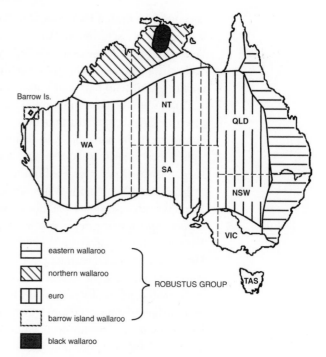

At one time the species *M. robustus* was divided into ten subspecies, largely on the basis of colour variations and small variations in morphology. However, Barry Richardson and Geoff Sharman, then at the University of New South Wales, used both molecular genetics and traditional skull and teeth measurements to determine that there are four distinct subspecies within *M. robustus* (Fig. 2.4). The eastern wallaroo, *M. robustus robustus*, is common on the eastern and western slopes of the Great Dividing Range. The euro or inland wallaroo, *M. r. erubescens*, is found over much of the drier areas of the continent. The northern wallaroo, *M. r. woodwardi*, is spread across north-western Australia from the Gulf of Carpentaria to the Kimberley region. A distinct small subspecies, *M. r. isabellinus*, lives on Barrow Island off the coast of northern Western Australia. There are morphological and physiological differences between the eastern wallaroo and the euro which are related to their different environments. The subspecies are separated geographically by the wide plains of the Darling River and its tributaries. At the north of this river basin, in central Queensland, the two subspecies do come together and over small distances animals can be seen that are difficult to place. Genetically the forms seem to merge and hybridisation is suspected in this area. Eastern wallaroos and euros do interbreed in captivity and the hybrids are fertile.

*Figure 2.4*
*Distribution of wallaroos and the euro in Australia. After Richardson and Sharman (1976).*

### EASTERN WALLAROO, *M. ROBUSTUS ROBUSTUS*

The eastern wallaroo is found on the eastern and western slopes of the Great Dividing Range from southern New South Wales to at least as far north as Cooktown in Queensland (Fig. 2.4).

*Description* As mentioned, eastern wallaroos are robust kangaroos, especially the males which have very solid shoulders and forearms. Male eastern wallaroos are usually dark grey to almost black in colour (Plate 6), while females are more variable but generally bluish grey with a lighter underside. In the more western parts of the eastern wallaroo's range some males may be a dark rusty brown. Eastern wallaroos have noticeably small ears, in contrast to the inland euros with their large expressive ears.

*Distribution and status* The eastern wallaroo is an inhabitant of rocky hill country of the Great Dividing Range and associated ranges that run the length of the eastern coast of Australia. The country is well watered and the rocky hills are used as refuges from predation. In its rough habitats there appear to be very secure populations. Individuals move out of rough country to feed on adjoining cleared pasture land. Whether the increase in pasture has favoured an increase in the eastern wallaroo population is unknown, but likely.

The biology of eastern wallaroos found at two sites in the New England tablelands of New South Wales was examined by Robert Taylor during his PhD work at the University of New England. The densities of eastern wallaroos at the two sites were markedly different and apparently associated with the degree of pasture improvement. The Lara site was fertilised and much 'improved' and eastern wallaroo average densities were 55 per km², while at the 'unimproved' Newholme site the density was only 8 per km². The high densities at the Lara site are unusual and rarely observed for any kangaroo species in Australia. Taylor also compared the responses of eastern wallaroos and grey kangaroos to disturbance while they were feeding. The grey kangaroos usually moved off together in a coordinated manner, while the eastern wallaroos more often than not scattered in many directions and headed in ones and twos toward sheltering habitat.

## EURO OR INLAND WALLAROO, *M. ROBUSTUS ERUBESCENS*

The first major study of the field biology of a kangaroo was carried out on the euro. The decline of the wool industry in the arid Pilbara district of Western Australia in the 1940s and 1950s was said to be due to euros competing with the sheep for feed. The study, conducted by Tim Ealey of CSIRO, showed that it was poor management, with continued overgrazing by sheep, that was the problem. All the same, much valuable information about the biology of euros was obtained.

*Description* Adult male euros are 'chunky' medium-sized kangaroos, with relatively large ears (Plate 7). The largest males that I have encountered were just 52 kg. The females are small delicate animals (Plate 8). The colour of this subspecies is highly variable, shifting from dark grey (similar to the eastern wallaroo) in the east of its range to a deep rusty red colour in Western Australia. Females tend to be somewhat lighter in colour, particularly underneath. At Fowlers Gap Research Station in western New South Wales the colours tend to be intermediate between eastern and western forms and highly variable. Females may be a light sandy grey to dark rusty grey, with males being light grey to dark rusty grey.

*Distribution and status* The euro is found in the drier areas of the continent, wherever there is suitable rough habitat. It extends from central western New South Wales and Queensland west to the Indian Ocean coast. Euros are abundant, although their distribution is patchy due to their habitat preferences. In some areas populations have increased in recent times, notably in Western Australia, while there are suggestions that numbers have declined in more settled regions. Euros can exist in large numbers but are difficult to count. In a hilly area at Fowlers Gap aerial survey counts suggested a population size of 200–300. However, in a capture-mark-release study at a waterhole the population was estimated to be eight to ten times larger. Ground counts in the Pilbara have given similar population densities: around 10–15 euros per km$^2$. Large variations often occur between sites and with changing environmental conditions (Fig. 2.5).

The euro and other wallaroos do not seem to be under much threat from humans at present or in the foreseeable future. Euros are not exploited to a significant degree by commercial harvesting. They make up only about 3 per cent of the overall commercial quota for macropods. This is due to the rough country in which they live and because they are generally smaller than other kangaroos. Euros are also regarded more benignly by landholders than are the red or grey kangaroos. The secretive nature of the euro leads to underestimations of population size, and a female euro feeding quietly among the rocks is a pretty little animal unlikely to attract a shooter's attention.

**Figure 2.5**
*Variations in euro density with rainfall patterns (seasonal totals shown in columns) and between sites. South Ridge site ( ■ ) at Fowlers Gap Station is prime habitat and has many more mature females than South Sandstone site ( □ ). High densities in South Ridge in 1984 and early 1985 reflect a breeding surge after the end of the 1982–83 drought. The big increase at both sites in winter 1986 was not due to changes in breeding or mortality but to an influx from surrounding areas, due to rain after a dry period being localised on the hills of Fowlers Gap. After Clancy and Croft (1992).*

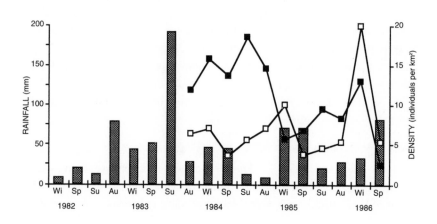

## NORTHERN WALLAROO, M. *ROBUSTUS WOODWARDI*

This wallaroo from northern Australia was recently classified as a sub-species of *Macropus robustus* rather than a separate species. As with other macropods of the far north of Australia our knowledge of it is still rudimentary, but is increasing rapidly.

*Description* In colour and appearance northern wallaroos are more like the euros of Western Australia, in that the males are typically reddish rather than dark grey; the females are a light rusty grey. The morphology of northern wallaroos is similar to that of euros, but distinct genetic differences occur. It is not known whether they grade into the euro type in the southern part of their range or whether there is a geographic gap separating the subspecies. When it comes to identification in the field there are some problems in distinguishing the females from those of black wallaroos and antilopine kangaroos, which can occur in the same regions. Generally, the black wallaroos are smaller, about two-thirds the size, and darker. The antilopine kangaroos tend to be more rusty in colour. Experienced field biologists can easily tell the species apart, but they have a feel for the 'whole animal'.

*Distribution and status* Northern wallaroos are found across the Top End of Australia, from the Kimberley region in the west to the Arnhem Land plateau and the Gulf of Carpentaria in the east (Fig. 2.4). Working in Kakadu National Park, Tony Press noted that the northern wallaroo and the black wallaroo were found together on scree slopes on the Arnhem Land escarpment. On the foot slopes and nearby floodplains northern wallaroos were seen with antilopine kangaroos, particularly at night. The underlying basis for this overlap in habitat is not yet understood. Generally, where other species overlap, when the microhabitats are examined in detail the level of potential competition is found to be low.

Details of population size of northern wallaroos are not available. It is only around the Darwin area (including Kakadu National Park) that there is some indication of densities. On the edge of the Arnhem Land escarpment densities of northern wallaroos rarely average more than 1 per km$^2$, much lower than that of the black wallaroo in this area. In a hilly site 80 km south of Darwin David Croft found densities of 3–4 per km$^2$, but even there, in their prime habitat, these relatively solitary animals were outnumbered by antilopine kangaroos.

## BARROW ISLAND WALLAROO, M. *ROBUSTUS ISABELLINUS*

A distinct subspecies of the 'robustus' group of wallaroos lives on Barrow Island, a faunistically interesting island off the coast of northern Western Australia (Fig. 2.4). This Barrow Island wallaroo, *M. r. isabellinus*, is shorter and stockier in build than the other subspecies and reaches not much more than half the size of adults of the other subspecies. Males are buffy red on the back.

*Distribution and status* The ancestors of these animals were cut off from the mainland 12,000–13,500 years ago when the sea level rose after the ending of the last glacial period. Genetic changes associated with the isolation of a relatively small population led to rapid divergence from the mainland form. The island is currently a nature reserve and protection levels seem adequate. However, it is in the nature of island populations to be fragile and we can only hope that this little euro is relatively secure in its status.

## BLACK WALLAROO, *MACROPUS BERNARDUS*

The black wallaroo is very much the unknown kangaroo of Australia, but it is clearly specifically distinct from the wallaroos of the 'robustus' group (Plate 9). This small wallaroo, about two-thirds the size of the northern wallaroo, is found in a limited area on the edge of the Arnhem Land escarpment. It is a distinctive kangaroo both in morphology and genetics. It has 18 chromosomes against 16 for the other kangaroos (except the red kangaroo, which has 20).

*Description* The black wallaroo is the smallest of the kangaroos, except for the diminutive Barrow Island wallaroo. The name of this little wallaroo is somewhat misleading since only the males are darkly coloured. Males are sooty brown to glossy black, while females are dark brown to greyish. The belly of the female is light. The ears are generally shorter than those of the northern wallaroos that may be found in the vicinity. The muzzle pattern is similar to that of members of the 'robustus' group (Fig. 2.1).

*Distribution and status* Black wallaroos are restricted to a small area of western and central Arnhem Land (Fig. 2.4). Their habitat is the steep rocky escarpments of this region, in areas where the northern wallaroo and the antilopine kangaroo are also seen. The diversity of wallaroo 'types' in the Top End of Australia has led to the suggestion that the group evolved in this region and spread from there to much of the rest of Australia. The black wallaroo is more limited in distribution than these other species are but in the core of its range it is common. In extensive helicopter surveys made by Tony Press around Kakadu National Park the black wallaroo was seen only on the sandstone escarpment and plateau of Arnhem Land and its outliers. It was most commonly seen in heavily dissected sandstone country with a variety of vegetation types, including tropical monsoon forest. During the surveys black wallaroos were most often seen singly or in twos or threes, but on one occasion 12 black wallaroos were observed grazing together in spinifex hummock grassland within the escarpment.

The black wallaroo is regarded as being extremely wary and difficult to approach. I know of several researchers who have been keen to observe this animal, but even after much scrambling among the rocks of 'prime habitat' they, like me, have come away with only glimpses. The black wallaroo's average density on the Arnhem Land escarpment is probably about 0.6 per km$^2$, but in patches of monsoon forest in the dissected escarpment densities of 1.5–2.5 per km$^2$ may occur.

## ANTILOPINE KANGAROO, *Macropus antilopinus*

The antilopine kangaroo occurs in the monsoonal tropical woodlands of northern Australia. While it is sometimes referred to as the antilopine wallaroo it does not strictly belong in that group. It is more like the red and grey kangaroos in behaviour and habitat use. John Gould in 1863 was much taken by 'the Red Wallaroo of the Cobourg Peninsula' (Plate 10). He described it as a noble species, second only in colour and form to the red kangaroo. Antilopine kangaroos are slender and long-limbed, as befits their mobile lifestyle. Their common name comes from their supposed likeness in colouration and fur texture to antelopes.

*Description* Although the antilopine kangaroos are most closely related to the wallaroos and the euro, in outward appearance they more resemble the grey and red kangaroos. In the Northern Territory they are often known as 'red kangaroos'. Male antilopine kangaroos are reddish tan above and much paler on the front or undersurface. The tips of the paws and hind feet are black. The females are more variable in colour. They usually have a pale grey head and forequarters but the rest of the back may be all grey or reddish tan, like the males. Males have a very characteristic swelling of the nose behind the nostrils. This enlargement of the nasal passages is probably related to the need to lose heat by panting in this hot climate: kangaroos pant through their nose with their mouth closed. Antilopine kangaroos have a muzzle skin pattern similar to that of wallaroos (Fig. 2.1). Gould's collector, John Gilbert, took a male of 55 kg and commented that some males were in excess of 70 kg. The relatively small size of the females was also noted by Gould. A female of 30 kg is considered to be big.

*Hopping profile* When hopping the antilopine kangaroos hold themselves similarly to grey kangaroos, but the stockier build is noticeable.

*Distribution and status* This is the kangaroo of the savannah woodlands of northern tropical Australia. It is found in a broad band from the Kimberley region of Western Australia to the Gulf of Carpentaria and then again in the open eucalyptus forests on Cape York (Fig. 2.4). Whether it occurs in the grasslands across the bottom of the Gulf of

Carpentaria is debated. A lack of genetic differences between the Arnhem Land and Cape York populations suggests that there is interchange between the two.

The population size and conservation status of the antilopine kangaroo are unclear. It is regarded as being common, especially within the western part of its range. A good estimate of population size is difficult to obtain, given the remoteness of the region and the limited work done on the species. David Croft of the University of New South Wales undertook a study of the socio-ecology of the macropods some 80km south of Darwin and included antilopine kangaroos. He examined two sites in both wet and dry seasons, one hilly with narrow valleys and one flatter with open grassy depressions, which were inundated in the wet season. When the antilopine kangaroos were in the hilly site they were found on ridge tops and valley floors, but they tended to avoid steep-sided rocky ridges with thick scrub, where northern wallaroos were most common. The densities of antilopine kangaroos were much higher on the open site in both wet and dry seasons, reaching 31 per km$^2$ during the wet season. The densities in the hilly site were about a third of this. Overall, these densities are high when compared to those of other species of kangaroos elsewhere, but whether such densities are widespread is unclear.

# SOCIAL ORGANISATION

## GROUP ORGANISATION

Hundreds of red kangaroos moving with beautiful grace across the open plains of the outback; dozens of grey kangaroos bounding effortlessly through open forest — these are common impressions. Such scenes do occur, but they are not representative of the usual pattern of life of kangaroos. Kangaroos do not move around much, not even the red kangaroos of the interior; they are generally sedentary and once they reach maturity they may live out their lives in home-ranges that are only a couple of kilometres across. Kangaroos are social animals but usually associate in small groups of less than half a dozen individuals. These groups consist mainly of females and their young, particularly daughters. The large mobs of grey kangaroos and red kangaroos that may be seen from the late afternoon through to early morning are loose feeding aggregations of animals, which are concentrating in a preferred feeding site.

The reasons for social structure are several. Sexual interaction is a primary one, but more about that later. Another obvious reason is increased protection from predation. The more eyes watching for predators the safer the individual. This may be one focus for the common small groups. A study made by Peter Jarman in the New England tablelands found that the rate at which eastern grey kangaroos entered and left a group was influenced by the size of the group. When only a few animals were present they tended to stick together and to be more vigilant (Fig. 3.1). Also, there is the point of 'knowing your neighbours'. Most mammals have a need to restrict the number of individuals regularly encountered to a manageable, recognisable level. Frequent meetings with strangers, with whom no social relationships have been established, are stressful and wasteful in time and energy.

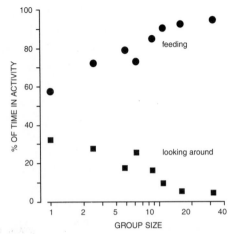

While the continuing bonds between mothers and daughters are important for group cohesion, a low level of aggression is also important for the maintenance of group structure. Among the more gregarious species there is tolerance of young animals in the groups and, importantly, adult males are (mostly) tolerant of each other. Continuing interaction within a mob or group also allows kangaroos to establish dominance hierarchies, thereby reducing possibly damaging interaction. This is not only the case with adult males in potential breeding situations but is true for both sexes, since more dominant females will displace other females and small males from shade and feed.

It is helpful to understand some of the terms used in the study of social structure. When talking about kangaroos many workers use the term 'group'. In this connection a group is taken to mean a number of animals observed in substantially closer proximity to one another than to other members of the population. Members of a group are potentially able to communicate and interact cohesively. Some researchers restrict membership of a group to those animals within a specified distance of a neighbour, say 50 metres; that is, those animals able to communicate visually. In practice field workers have little difficulty telling which animals belong to a particular group. Oddly, a lone animal is considered a group of one.

Other terms in which researchers have discussed the social organisation of kangaroos include 'aggregation' and 'mob'. These terms give insight into the structure of kangaroo populations at a local level.

An aggregation encompasses kangaroos concentrated in response to a resource (feed, water, shade, etc.) but not necessarily interacting cohesively. Field workers often use this term when referring to a large body of kangaroos whose real social structure is unknown. Aggregations are often noted close to *sporadic* food resources, such as in an area where an isolated thunderstorm has produced localised green feed during a drought.

A mob is a set of individuals whose home-ranges overlap, which commonly interact and all of which may associate. It may be rare to find all

***Figure 3.1***
*Vigilance (looking around) by individual eastern grey kangaroos decreases during feeding periods when group size increases. In bigger groups a kangaroo has more actual foraging time. After Jarman and Coulson (1989).*

members of a mob together at one time. Among grey kangaroos the term mob is applied to the consistent large groups that feed in a specific area over time. The mob is the long-term pool of associates among which the individual leads its social life. One mob is distinguished from another by non-overlapping home-ranges or lack of association between respective members. Young animals and a few adults may disperse and enter different mobs.

A 'group', as discussed, refers to the current social neighbourhood of an individual; that is, the number and density of fellows with which it is interacting. 'Subgroups' can be distinguished within a group if the group is well understood. Several studies have been able to detail such subgroups in which sets of animals are closer to, and interact more with, each other than the rest of the group. Subgroups may persist over months or years. With kangaroos, subgroups tend to be regarded as having the features of 'closed-membership groups'. The usual groups of kangaroos are 'open-membership groups' and their composition can change from hour to hour or from day to day through the comings and goings of individuals. It is a pity that we do not have better terms for these social structures but we have only recently begun to understand them. The jargon will come in time.

**Table 3.1**

Level of gregariousness in kangaroo species as indicated by mean and typical group size

| Species | Mean group size | Range of group size | Typical group size |
|---|---|---|---|
| Antilopine | 4.6 | 2.2–5.4 | 3.3–11.7 |
| Eastern grey | 4.0 | 2.5–12.5 | 3.2–22.9 |
| Eastern grey (Tas.) | 3.6 | – | 5.4 |
| Western grey | 3.2 | 2.0–6.3 | 1.8–16.1 |
| Red | 2.5 | 2.2–2.6 | 3.4–3.9 |
| Eastern wallaroo | 2.0 | 1.8–2.2 | 2.6–3.6 |
| Euro | 2.1 | 1.4–2.3 | 2.2–2.6 |
| Northern wallaroo | 1.1 | 1.0–1.1 | 1.0–1.3 |

Gregariousness of a species is usually gauged by the size of its groups. Table 3.1 ranks the various species and subspecies in terms of average group size. Also included is 'typical' group size, which is a measure of the group in which the average individual occurs. This measure was introduced by Peter Jarman to give a better reflection of the social experience of individual animals. It is not necessary to go into the formula but, in practice, typical group size is approximately equal to the average group size plus one standard deviation. The variation in values given in Table 3.1 is due to several factors, not least the amount of work done so far on the species or subspecies. Importantly, however, social structure varies with density of animals and with environmental conditions. This is indicated in Fig. 3.2 where group size is plotted against animal density. The overall pattern to emerge is that antilopine kangaroos are most social, followed by the eastern grey. The wallaroo group would seem to contain the least social kangaroos.

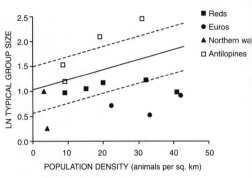

## ANTILOPINE KANGAROOS

Our most gregarious kangaroos, antilopines (Plate 10) may be seen lying together in close contact when resting, but this is unusual among other kangaroos. In open country south of Darwin antilopine kangaroos have been estimated to have a mean group size of about five animals. The underlying basis of these groups is not well understood, but they seem to be structured around females and their offspring. Large feeding aggregations (groups of groups?) of more than 10, and up to 50 animals were also common.

The social organisation of antilopine kangaroos can vary with habitat. David Croft found that females formed the bulk of the population in flatter, open areas, which are more productive. In this habitat in the wet season they outnumbered males 2:1; in the dry season 3:1. Of the adult males present, big males predominated. These were in mixed sex groups or alone as they moved through the habitat looking for females with signs of oestrus. Subadults of both sexes were present and associated with their own class and with females, presumably their mothers. Unlike the picture seen in other species, antilopine females with small young at foot were not normally removed from their usual group. In a hilly site there were equal numbers of females and males, but the adult males tended to be only medium-sized (20–60 kg). These males were often alone or in groups with other males. It seems that large males 'push' these smaller adult males out of the productive flatter areas, where females concentrate.

## EASTERN GREY KANGAROOS

Eastern greys are also relatively gregarious kangaroos. A mother and her young of recent years make up the core unit, and groups of 2–3 individuals are often seen in many habitats. Groupings of eastern grey kangaroos moving between resting and grazing sites generally vary between 2 and 10 individuals, with 3–4 being a common group unless density is high in the area. The relatedness of such sets of individuals is not clear but it is obvious that individuals know each other. Eleven females and their young consistently fed as a subgroup for many months at Bago State Forest in the highlands

*Figure 3.2*
*The effect of the density of kangaroos in an area on the 'typical' size of their groups; group size being plotted as the natural logarithm. The eastern grey kangaroo is used as the baseline. Antilopine kangaroos are most social, while wallaroos and euros appear least social. Based on Croft (1987), with additional information on red kangaroos and euros provided by Graeme Moss and Debbie Ashworth respectively.*

of southern New South Wales (Fig. 3.5). Large mobs may occur if productivity is high and if the kangaroos are not subject to heavy predation (from humans or dingos). At Bago State Forest up to 80 individuals of all size/sex classes were regularly observed in one such mob, the 'Sandy Creek mob', by Renata Jaremovic and David Croft. Several distinct large mobs were found spread through the area.

At Fowlers Gap Research Station, at the other end of the species' climatic range in far western New South Wales, eastern grey kangaroos are only observed in small groups, usually 1–4 individuals. Larger mobs do not form, apparently because of the low food levels. The largest groups seen along Fowlers Gap Creek have been mixed age/sex groups of 6–8 individuals. Along some 17 km of creekline three or four groups are seen. These animals are often sedentary, being seen in the same patch of timber through many seasons. A few animals, however, have been noted to change groups or move entirely out of the district.

Seasonal changes take place in the social structure of eastern grey kangaroos. At Bago State Forest large and presumably dominant males separated themselves from the main mobs in winter. This is when the seasonal breeding females are unlikely to come into oestrus. This is also the time when there is minimal pasture growth in the southern highlands of New South Wales and it would be beneficial for the mob to expand their overall foraging area. The big males in these groups tend to maintain more space vis-a-vis their neighbours than do the animals in the mixed sex groups.

## WESTERN GREY KANGAROOS

There are many similarities between the social organisation of western grey kangaroos and that of eastern grey kangaroos. Knowledge about the social organisation of western greys comes largely from two recent studies. One, by Grahame Arnold and co-workers at CSIRO, focused on wandoo gum woodland patches at Bakers Hill, near Northam, in the wheat belt of Western Australia. The other study was carried out at Kinchega National Park in western New South Wales by the State's National Parks and Wildlife Service and CSIRO.

As western grey kangaroos observed in the first study moved between daytime home-ranges in the wandoo woodland patches and their feeding grounds in farmland, their group sizes varied from 1 to 14. The mean group size was near 3 with the 'typical' group size being about 6. Again, adult females were the core of each group. Young animals tended to associate with other animals, often their mothers. Females tended to be with other females, young and juveniles. In feeding areas the composition of mobs, especially larger ones, was variable and changing. Despite this there were patterns of association in the loose groupings of adult females, with some females being pivotal in the groups. The role of such females in dominance patterns is not yet established.

At Bakers Hill one or two adult males were regularly in contact with such female-orientated groups and were possibly the dominant males. The other general loose association was between a few mature males, but associations are not long-lasting and vary from year to year. At Kinchega National Park males associated in groups in autumn and winter, the period of minimal breeding, as was the case with eastern grey kangaroos at Bago State Forest. These male groups may be important in establishing the dominance patterns among their members. Fighting is significant in these groups.

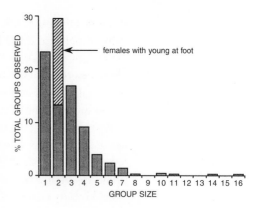

*Figure 3.3*
*Frequency with which red kangaroos at Fowlers Gap Station are found in different size groups. A total of 1174 animals were sighted in 613 groups. The number of female/young at foot groups contributing to the group size of two is shown. After Croft (1980).*

## RED KANGAROOS

Red kangaroos appear less social than antilopine and grey kangaroos, but their lower density may enhance this impression. Several studies of group-size distribution at Fowlers Gap Research Station in western New South Wales, which is 'good' red kangaroo habitat, showed a consistent picture (Fig. 3.3). During daylight David Croft found that 80 per cent of animals were in groups of two or more. The mean group size noted was 2.2–2.6 animals, with the typical group size being 3.7. Using a low-light video camera, Duncan Watson and I recorded similar values and found no difference in group size between day and night even though the animals were most active at night. In areas where red kangaroo densities are low, such as poor habitats or where heavy predation occurs, group sizes tend to be even lower. On the other hand, mobs of red kangaroos (10–20 animals) can be seen in good feeding areas and around clumps of shade trees. Larger aggregations may occur around patchy green feed and isolated waterholes.

Groups of red kangaroos are flexible and whether there are distinct sub-groups (apart from mother and young associations) is unclear. Although the pattern of red kangaroos joining and leaving a group throughout a day is irregular, stability in the short term is maintained, for example while going to and from water. As with the other kangaroos the group is not a random association; it is made up of local residents that are likely to be relatives and/or neighbours. There is social interaction and a form of hierarchy. This is easily seen in captive colonies but is harder to discern in the wild. The mature females are the hub of the social organisation, in that attention is focused upon them. They attract the males and stand aloof from young and immature individuals, except their own offspring. The large dominant males, like those of other species, are more likely to be found alone and are less likely to be in all-male groups than the medium-sized males are. The smaller immature males are most often found in mixed groups or in continued association with their mother.

Females with small young at foot are often separated from other groups. This pattern is seen in all other species except the antilopine kangaroos. Such behaviour is surprising because the mother and young would be expected to benefit from the watchfulness of a larger group. It has been argued that this is an indication of low levels of predation, but it is more likely to serve an anti-predator role: the young being more secure when hidden away with the mother. This may be compared with the new-born phase of many large social mammals, where the mother keeps the small and weak young away from the herd in which it would be an obvious focus for a fast predator.

There are other reasons why it would be beneficial for the mother and small young to be relatively solitary. When panicked in a mob the small young can lose contact with its mother. It is possible that isolation enables the small young to easily recognise and follow its mother in times of emergency. Support for this idea comes from Robert Taylor's work on eastern wallaroos. Females with young at foot specifically avoided other adult females when in larger groups. The mother–young pair also has a limited area of activity: the limited ability of the young to get around probably restricts the pair to a small region of the mother's home-range. A high quality patch of the home-range would presumably be chosen in such circumstances.

## EUROS

Euros and wallaroos are the least social of the kangaroos. Given that euros are very sedentary and have overlapping home-ranges, it is likely that the individuals in groups are well known to each other. Their group size was studied at Fowlers Gap Research Station where it was found to be 2.1, with the typical size being 2.6 animals. Apart from groups of males around oestrus females, larger groups (mobs?) are seen generally in prime feeding areas and around resting sites, such as rocky outcrops and caves in summer and shrubby gullies in winter. During a study involving radio-tracking, Tim Clancy found that in more open undulating country grouping tended to be higher than in more rugged country. This may help to increase awareness of predators or may perhaps be related to a concentration of resources. Patterns of association were not different between day and night, except in summer conditions when the euros were more social at night. At Fowlers Gap, which is prime habitat for euros, females with young at foot or subadult offspring were the most common social units seen.

Large males are commonly solitary when not associating with females. On the other hand, there are associations between non-dominant, mainly medium-sized, adult males, as seen seasonally in the grey kangaroos. Euros are not seasonal breeders, but due to the environmental unpredictability of the euro's habitat there are periods when many females are not breeding and male groupings are then more common. As with other species there is much fighting in these groups, since the males appear to have come together to sort out their positions in the social hierarchy.

## EASTERN WALLAROOS

The relatively solitary nature of eastern wallaroos parallels that of their inland relatives, with the mean group size in the New England tablelands being near 2. In that area the study done by Robert Taylor showed that almost 50 per cent of the individuals were alone; if females with small young at foot had been treated as one individual the pattern would have been more extreme. Notably, there was only a small effect of animal density on group size among the wallaroos. The 'improved' Lara site had wallaroo numbers of 55 per km$^2$, while at the 'unimproved' Newholme site the density was 8 per km$^2$. Despite the much higher density on Lara it was only in late afternoon, when feeding aggregations formed, that differences in group size occurred between Lara (2.2 animals per group), and Newholme (1.8 wallaroos per group), the typical group sizes being 3.6 and 2.6, respectively.

Large males, when not alone, are often found in the company of females with small young at foot. Such females are the most likely to enter oestrus in the near future, just after the young permanently leaves the pouch. Medium-sized males tend to be kept away from such females by the large males. As with euros the medium males tend to socialise with each other more than other sets of animals do and again much ritualised fighting takes place at such times.

The impact of possible predation on group structure is seen even in these less social kangaroos. Independent young animals (subadults) of both sexes were found to be alone least often of all social classes. Subadults are vulnerable to predation, and association with other individuals is beneficial in increasing detection of predators. Adult eastern wallaroos signal with a distinctive alarm foot thump when disturbed. Generally, association with adults is beneficial for subadults because of the experience the adults have of an area, especially when it comes to the distribution and quality of food and shelter. While adults tolerate subadults in their vicinity, the latter are soon rebuffed if they come too close. A hit or a sharp grunt will quickly encourage a young animal to keep its distance.

## OTHER WALLAROOS

The small amount of information available on the social organisation of the northern wallaroo, Barrow Island wallaroo and black wallaroo indicates that they follow the basic pattern known for the euro and eastern wallaroo. Northern wallaroos are generally solitary. In the South Alligator River area 78 per cent of sightings were of solitary individuals while the largest group

was only of three animals. In helicopter surveys of the sandstone escarpment and plateau of Arnhem Land and its outliers Tony Press noted that
black wallaroos were most often to be seen singly or in twos or threes; however, a mob of 12 grazing black wallaroos was recorded in spinifex hummock grassland within the Arnhem Land escarpment.

# HOME-RANGE, HABITAT USE AND ACTIVITY PATTERNS

Kangaroos are generally sedentary and confine their activities to familiar
areas: home-ranges. Under some conditions animals may disperse away
from their home-ranges and move long distances, but such events do not
represent the usual day-to-day scene and will be discussed in the next
chapter. Home-ranges are the areas that are covered by kangaroos in their
normal activities of feeding, mating and caring for young. For kangaroos
these areas are not 'territories' because they do not appear to be defended.
Good information on home-ranges is generally available only for mature,
established breeding animals. These are the core of the population and
their behaviour determines its overall structure. Subadults and young
adults may travel more.

A home-range may have relatively fixed boundaries, which can be centred on a feature such as an area of good pasture or, for euros, a hill with
good caves; or the home-range may gradually change over weeks or months.
Such 'drifting' home-ranges are more often seen in open country. The factors that influence changes in home-range are many and include changes
in food supply and environmental conditions. Seasonal changes in food
supply also can lead to the expansion and contraction of the home-range.
Not all areas in a home-range are used equally; there are core areas of
greater importance and regions that the kangaroo uses rarely or when moving between the significant areas.

There has been some disagreement among biologists as to how a home-
range should be measured. Estimates given for a species by different workers often are not easily compared. Recent techniques give an estimate of
the general breadth of the home-range and of its core use area. One form
of these estimates is 'minimum areas used at different probability levels',
called MAP values. MAP(95) represents the smallest area that accounts for
95 per cent of the utilisation distribution at the time under investigation,
and is used to describe the total home-range. MAP(50) is used as an index
of the core area, i.e. the area of intensive use within the home-range.

The best techniques for studying home-ranges and movements involve
the tracking of animals fitted with small radio transmitters on collars
(Fig. 4.4 & Plate 11). The tracking can be done by 'hand' tracking or by
fixed station tracking. In hand tracking the researcher uses a small

**Figure 3.4**
*One of the tracking
stations on the
open plains of
Fowlers Gap
Research Station.
Radio-collared red
kangaroos are being
tracked by David
Croft and his
students via the
directional receiving
antennas. (Photo
David Croft.)*

directional antenna and walks around to locate the kangaroo and mark its position on a detailed map. In open country vehicles or even planes can be used for hand tracking. Signal strength from a radio transmitter is much reduced by trees and hilly ground so that tracking animals such as grey kangaroos in forest is very difficult, and almost impossible at night.

Fixed station tracking involves setting up two or more fixed receiving stations, usually at geographic high points or in towers. The stations are fitted with large, accurate, directional receiving antennas (Fig. 3.4). Compass bearings to an animal are simultaneously taken at specific times.

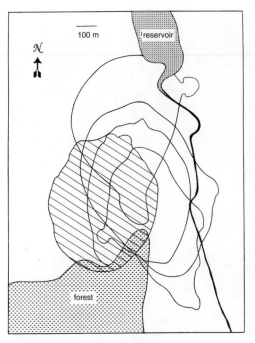

100 m

ℵ

reservoir

forest

**Figure 3.5**
*Home-ranges of
adult female eastern
grey kangaroos in
the vicinity of Bago
State Forest and
Blowering Reservoir,
southern highlands
of New South
Wales. Indicated
are long-term 95
per cent use areas
of animals at
morning and
evening activity
periods. The diag-
onally hatched area
represents the
nearly identical
home-ranges of a
cohesive subgroup
of eleven females.
Home-ranges of
some other females
in the 'Sandy Creek
mob' are also shown.
After Jaremovic and
Croft (1991).*

The animal is located by triangulation and its position plotted repeatedly. Animals can be tracked over 24 hours, if enough 'volunteer' trackers are available. This technique has been used successfully in open country, particularly where there are isolated hills in open plains. It is not successful in rough forest country because of attenuation of the transmitter signals by trees and hills. In this type of country 'hand' tracking using light planes has been used but this can give only a general picture of broad movements. Tracking via satellites is developing but fine resolution is not yet possible. It is still very expensive; however, it is the technique of the future.

## EASTERN GREY KANGAROOS

Because eastern grey kangaroos are animals of the forest and woodland comprehensive information on their home-ranges is sparse. They generally rest in cover during the middle of the day and they may feed within their forest or woodland habitats. Open areas have a much higher production of grass, the principal feed of grey kangaroos, and they often leave cover to forage in the open, sometimes in large numbers. It is in these conditions that information on home-ranges and movements can be more readily obtained.

In such conditions the 'activity' home-ranges of the eastern grey kangaroo are surprisingly small. At Bago State Forest the MAP(95)s of eleven tagged females closely overlapped (Fig. 3.5). During the study made by Renata Jaremovic and David Croft of the University of New South Wales the average value was 20 hectares (range 12.7–36.8 ha) and the outer boundary of the combined home-range of this subgroup was 26.6 ha. The full home-ranges, including the forest resting sites, were probably not much larger since there were many 'hip holes' just inside the forest's edge. This pattern was maintained for some three years. Other females had home-ranges that partly overlapped those of this subgroup, but observation indicated that they did not belong to the cohesive subgroup. While some males also occupied a similar home-range, others overlapped but had about double the ranges. A few other males moved their core areas significantly during the year. One large male moved regularly between two centres of activity, which were 5 km apart. Generally, big males moved more than smaller mature males, which may reflect their higher feeding needs or their greater reproductive activity.

The small home-ranges at Bago State Forest may be due to the high productivity of the area which consists of abandoned improved pasture.

Information from sites in the New England region of New South Wales suggests that home-ranges there are bigger in less productive areas. One might expect that in the arid zone the home-ranges of eastern grey kangaroos would be larger due to the lower productivity. But limited information obtained at Fowlers Gap Research Station indicates that this is not always so; animals there were restricted to the vicinity of the limited cover along creeklines. These are also the more productive areas. The restricted movement of females with small young at foot is indicated by a 7.7 ha weekly home-range, MAP(95), of one such female at Fowlers Gap.

Kangaroos have generally been regarded as being crepuscular; that is, most active at dawn and dusk with periods of relative inactivity in the middle of the night as well as during the middle of the day. When researchers have been able to examine the situation with good night-vision equipment kangaroos turn out to be more nocturnal. Additionally, the eastern grey kangaroo in more typical habitats in eastern Australia can feed throughout the day. This is not so at the arid extremes of their range, at least in hotter months.

Eastern grey kangaroos studied at Wallaby Creek in the New England tablelands could be active at any time of the day (Fig. 3.6), but resting mostly occurred in the middle of the day. The time spent harvesting food varied with the season. It was 7.4 hours per day in summer and 14 hours per day in winter. The increase in winter was due in part to more time being spent harvesting the same amount of food as food quality decreased, and in part to a greater energy need in the cooler months. Male and female eastern grey kangaroos had similar feeding times but differed in other aspects of their daily activities. Males moved further in a day than did females, particularly in the later part of the night when they visited many different subgroups, presumably to check for oestrus females. Females rarely left their subgroup to contact others at this time.

## WESTERN GREY KANGAROOS

Home-range size and habitat use of western grey kangaroos has been examined in work at Bakers Hill in remnant woodland in the wheat country of Western Australia, and also in several studies in semi-arid areas of New

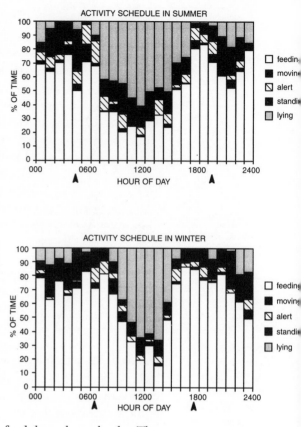

*Figure 3.6
Daily activity patterns during summer and winter of eastern grey kangaroos at Wallaby Creek in northern New South Wales. In both seasons some kangaroos could be feeding throughout the day. Feeding includes all associated activities, including moving while selecting feed. Arrows indicate sunrise and sunset. After Clarke et al. (1989).*

South Wales and Victoria. Although the environments are different the patterns of habitat use were found to be similar. Basically, there is a daytime core area that is used for shelter and concealment and a night-time feeding area. The latter may overlap the daytime area or it may be further away and distinct, such as a farm pasture.

Both patterns were seen at Bakers Hill. Western grey kangaroos spent most of the daytime in woodland with a shrub understorey but many moved out to feed in pasture at night. Values obtained by radio telemetry for the home-ranges were calculated differently from those given for the eastern grey kangaroo at Bago State Forest (NSW); however, the comparable home-ranges appear to be double those of the eastern grey. Females and smaller males occupied smaller areas than the larger males. Western grey kangaroos in Kinchega National Park showed a similar pattern but on a much larger scale, presumably because of the lower availability of food. The long-term home-range, MAP(95), as obtained over 20 months via tracking from fixed tracking stations, was around 400 hectares. On smaller time scales the average home-range decreased, being 213 ha during three-week periods in each season. The area used on a daily basis was generally about 100 ha.

The usual preference of western grey kangaroos for wooded country was also noted in the dry country of Kinchega National Park where they were associated with the wooded floodplain of the Darling River. Because of this the home-ranges of western greys did not change much as weather and pasture conditions changed. Red kangaroos in the area generally had similar home-ranges but these increased with increasing aridity. Similar patterns occur at Fowlers Gap. The close association of grey kangaroos with cover may be related to predation and/or protection from environmental extremes.

The broad pattern of daily activity and its variation with season was determined by radio telemetry at Kinchega National Park. Western grey kangaroos foraged for six to ten hours per day. The duration of grazing was similar in autumn, winter and spring, but was 22 per cent less in summer. This summer pattern may be due to the shorter nights and high daytime temperatures. Western grey kangaroos grazed through the night in summer but still grazed almost three hours less than the arid-adapted red kangaroo in this season. During the cooler seasons most western grey kangaroos were grazing two to three hours after sunset but grazing tapered off after about six hours. Another feeding period occurred some two hours before and after sunrise. The lull in feeding in the middle of the night was longer in winter.

Environmental conditions affect behaviour on a day-to-day basis. During a series of 24-hour observations of western grey kangaroos in a small enclosure in Western Australia the maximum daily temperatures ranged from 22.4°C to 42.3°C. While the general pattern of activity was similar to that seen at Kinchega National Park, grazing time was much reduced on the hottest days. During one day when the temperature reached 42.3°C animals started grazing 2.5 hours later in the evening and rested more during the night. All animals ceased grazing by 10 a.m. There were other environmental effects on the activity. The interaction between air temperature and sunshine affected the amount of resting time that was spent in the shade. Also, on windy days less time was spent in the shade.

## RED KANGAROOS

These dry-country kangaroos were considered to be nomadic, moving across the landscape to utilise patchy, variable resources. Indeed, work done by Tony Oliver in Western Australia in the mid-1960s was initiated to answer the question: Are red kangaroos so mobile that localised control efforts (shooting animals or poisoning of waterholes) would be frustrated by rapid reinvasion from distant areas? The matter has now been largely resolved but the answer is, of course, more complex than most workers anticipated.

Several long-term studies in western New South Wales and in Western Australia have involved tagging and radio tracking of red kangaroos. Of note were the studies of Peter Bailey and co-workers at Tero Creek Station (NSW), Martin Denny and helpers at Sturt National Park (NSW), the Kinchega National Park study done by Graeme Caughley and colleagues, the work of Tony Oliver and colleagues in Western Australia, and the Fowlers Gap study done by the School of Zoology, University of New South Wales; David Croft had a central role in the tracking aspects of the Fowlers Gap study. The latter two studies represent two extremes of the story. The work at Fowlers Gap was carried out in sheep country where water is readily available and red kangaroo numbers are at their highest; in contrast, the Western Australian study was in dry country where numbers were relatively low and where dingos were common.

An interesting insight into red kangaroo movements was provided by Tony Oliver. He noted that coat colours of males and females varied from district to district. The variations were often quite marked over small distances (Fig. 3.7), for example in the north-west of Western Australia. He argued that regional colour differences would not exist if there was a substantial movement and genetic interchange between localities. We now know that most red kangaroos are not nomadic. There is dispersal of many young, and some adults can move long distances (Chapter 4). However, most of the mature, breeding population are sedentary and once they become established in an area they live out their lives there. These animals may 'move camp' sometimes, but they generally show fidelity to their chosen area.

Characteristics of home-ranges obviously vary. The red kangaroo is an animal of the open plains and a typical habitat in the west of New South Wales is open grassland or shrubland with a few scattered clumps of trees or large shrubs to provide daytime shelter from the harsh sun (Fig. 8.2). But red kangaroos are widely spread throughout Australia and they may be found

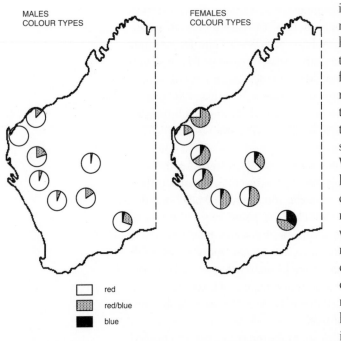

MALES
COLOUR TYPES

FEMALES
COLOUR TYPES

□ red
▦ red/blue
■ blue

*Figure 3.7*
*Coat colour variation in male and female red kangaroos of different districts in Western Australia. 'Red' includes shades from dark red/brown to sandy red/brown. 'Red/blue' ranges from almost blue to almost sandy red. Blue is blue/grey. Some morphs within these colour ranges appear distinct and were treated as such by Tony Oliver in his study. After Oliver (1986).*

in woodland on the floodplains of major rivers or on bare, stony low hills. In short, they can be found virtually anywhere there is sufficient feed and some shade. Red kangaroos are particularly economical in their water use and they may need to drink only every week or two in summer. In western New South Wales water is generally not a problem because it is provided for domestic stock. The reds' home-ranges may be well removed from water but they can quickly move many kilometres to reach it. In the cooler seasons they may not need to drink for many months. In the dry north-west of Western Australia home-ranges are usually based within 10–15 km of a water source.

Home-ranges of red kangaroos at Fowlers Gap have been determined by radio tracking. The average daily home-ranges, MAP(95), were around 150 hectares or 1.5 square kilometres. These did not vary much with the season and males did not use bigger areas than the females used. The core use areas, MAP(50), were roughly 20–35 per cent of the MAP(95) areas. Weekly home-ranges were two to three times larger than daily ranges, because red kangaroos tend to vary their daily resting sites. When ten kangaroos at Fowlers Gap were tracked over a week the maximum distances that such sites changed between days were 1.5–3.3 km. These values give a general idea of the dimensions of a red kangaroo's living area. Radio tracking done by Tony Oliver near Wiluna (WA) gave a similar picture. In all studies the animals' major regular excursions out of their home-ranges were to water points in hot summer conditions. The intervals between these excursions were usually 3–10 days.

It is still unclear whether home-ranges of red kangaroos overlap. In the WA studies mature females had exclusive use of their home-ranges, particularly the MAP(50) core area; but not at Kinchega National Park or Fowlers Gap in New South Wales. The different densities of red kangaroos in the two regions may explain this difference. The densities in western New South Wales are five to ten times higher than those at the sites examined in Western Australia. Further studies are needed before this explanation can be accepted.

The size of male home-ranges versus female home-ranges has implications for mating strategies. Although some studies suggest that males range more widely than females do, this does not seem to be the case for mature established individuals on a daily or weekly basis at Fowlers Gap. David Croft suggests that, within this time frame, rather than ranging widely in search for oestrus females large males centre their home-ranges in areas where oestrus females (often those with large pouch young) are likely to concentrate. These sites are those with the best feed and shelter. Such females may also advertise their status by increasingly moving around the edges of their home-range.

In a 20-month tracking study in the north-west of Western Australia, in which the animals were located each month, mature males changed their activity centres over a broader area than did the females. Males had discrete home-ranges during this time which were about twice the size of those of the females. In the longer term, mature males may range over wider areas than females do. The general picture of male movements is difficult to clarify because of differences in kangaroo density and in the size/status relationships of the males in different regions. The density of the population, and thus the density of breeding females, presumably has effects on the movement patterns of males.

The daily activities of red kangaroos focus on foraging. Apart from resting, other behaviours, even reproductive behaviour, make up only a small part of the average day. At Fowlers Gap Duncan Watson and I examined the pattern of daily activity over several seasons using a low-light video camera. Red kangaroos were most active at night and in the few hours after sunrise and before sunset. Resting was common around midday and early afternoon in all seasons; and in the late night hours, between midnight and dawn, in the colder months. While the duration of the daytime rest period increased from winter to spring and summer, the late night rest period contracted over the same period. Foraging activity mirrored the resting periods. A peak in foraging occurred at dawn in all seasons; presumably the kangaroos topped up their large forestomachs before resting for the day. The onset of feeding in the evening coincided with sunset. There was no peak of feeding at sunset; it was maintained into the night. Red kangaroos were not seen to drink in winter. In spring and summer most visits to water were at night. Of the minor activities grooming, especially thermoregulatory saliva spreading, accounted for most of the activity around midday in spring and summer. Of the other minor activities, digging hip holes and getting comfortable were significant in the middle of the day.

## EUROS

The strong association of euros with rocky hill country may simply be due to competition and natural selection. At Fowlers Gap Research Station euros appear at a competitive advantage in the hills, while red kangaroos have the advantage on the flat country. Would euros move off the hills if red kangaroos were removed from the plains? The picture in the Pilbara district of Western Australia suggests that this might be so. There, due to gross overgrazing by sheep, red kangaroos were largely eliminated from the plains. Subsequently, euros which have lower feed requirements than red kangaroos, increased their numbers and colonised the open country — and many did not use rocky outcrops for protection from heat if water was provided. Also, when heavy summer rain came many euros dispersed well away from the grazed-out area around the outcrops and permanent water; they lived on the open plains, sheltering in creeklines and under trees. If the sheep, stock water and dingo controls were all removed, presumably the euros would be pushed back into the hills and the red kangaroos would re-establish in numbers on the plains.

Yet studies of the home-ranges of euros in western New South Wales have tended to confirm their preference for rough hilly country. In his study at Fowlers Gap Station Tim Clancy especially noted this among females; they rarely shifted their home-ranges out of rocky country. Home-ranges of euros at Fowlers Gap were small and essentially stable over time, though there were some variations with seasonal conditions and landform. Daily home-ranges, MAP(95), averaged between 10 ha and 37 ha, with some euros ranging over an area as small as 1 ha in 24 hours. In contrast, the daily home-range of the red kangaroos on the adjacent plains at the same time was approximately 140 ha. Euros do not use all of their small home-ranges evenly. This is highlighted by the difference between the daily home-range, MAP(95), and the core area, MAP(50). A euro's core area was focused on the use of specific resting sites and was generally less than 20 per cent of its total home-range. The pattern of home-range use can vary with time. However, comparison of the daily, weekly and yearly home-ranges (Fig. 3.8) indicates how little the euros move about, especially the females. In the short term most euros show very strong fidelity to their home-ranges. Animals translocated 15–20 km away from their home-ranges return within days. Short-term movements to isolated rain events in droughts have been noted, however (Fig. 2.5).

**Figure 3.8**
*Size of home-ranges, MAP(95), of female and male euros at Fowlers Gap Station. As well as the measurement of yearly home-range, assessments were made in both summer and winter of daily and weekly home-ranges. Males ranged more widely in winter. Values are the averages for a three-year study. Derived from Clancy and Croft (1990).*

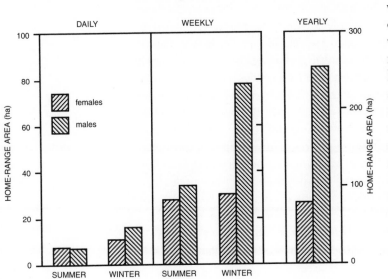

Interesting variations in levels of movement occur between the sexes in relation to season. The two sexes use similar home-range areas in summer but in winter the males range more widely (Fig. 3.8). This seasonal effect is greater for the weekly home-range than for the daily home-range. The net effect is that in winter the total weekly home-range of males, about 78 ha, is more than double that of females, 30 ha. The summer home-ranges of both sexes are also some 30 ha: males decrease their movements in summer due to the high temperatures. By having much larger home-ranges in other seasons the males overlap a number of female home-ranges, thereby increasing their potential reproductive success. The long-term home-ranges of individual euros at Fowlers Gap in most cases were focused on one area, and the pattern of overall movement did not change much from year to year. Tim Clancy and David Croft noted, though, that a small percentage of both males and females shifted their locations in such a way that their yearly home-range areas continually moved.

## EASTERN WALLAROOS

Wallaroos live in most of the rough country of the Great Dividing Range and its associated ranges in eastern Australia. On the western slopes in northern New South Wales wallaroos are typically found where rocky hills and gullies covered with open forest are interspersed with open pastures and wheat fields. Perhaps the most extreme habitats lie in the mountainous gorge country of the eastern scarp of the New England plateau. Within all these habitats the focus is on the availability of rocky refuges. Where rocky outcrops are small and isolated by pasture, large males tend to occupy them to the exclusion of medium-sized males. Oddly, females with small young at foot seem to avoid such places.

Details of wallaroo home-ranges are unknown, but Peter Jarman and Robert Taylor have provided some insights into movement patterns from their studies in the New England tablelands. The sedentary nature of eastern wallaroos, relative to eastern grey kangaroos, was indicated by the numbers of tagged animals that were resighted at least once within the two years following tagging. Eastern wallaroo males were resighted most frequently (84%), while 76 per cent of females were seen again. By comparison, 61 per cent of male and 54 per cent of female grey kangaroos were resighted. Frequently sighted eastern wallaroos, of both sexes, lived within small areas; the maximum distance between sightings being 0.4 km for a female and 0.9 km for a male. One radio-tracked female was observed over five months and she did not move beyond two kilometres from her capture site. Her movements centred on a rocky hill in pasture land and extended to, but not across, a small creek. The patterns of movement by eastern wallaroos appear very similar to those of euros.

## NORTHERN WALLAROOS

Northern wallaroos are generally solitary, and accordingly we tend to see a population dispersed through suitable habitat with small home-ranges. The MAP(95) for one male in the Adelaide River area of the Northern Territory was observed by David Croft to be only 10 ha; this wallaroo confined most of its activities to a single steep-sided rocky ridge with thick scrub. The steep rocky home-ranges of northern wallaroos may help them avoid predation from dingos, which are common in the area.

## ANTILOPINE KANGAROOS

In the area in which the northern wallaroos were studied David Croft also assessed home-ranges of antilopine kangaroos. While antilopines were close to the areas used by northern wallaroos they did not overlap noticeably with each other. Antilopine kangaroo home-ranges were significantly the larger. One medium-sized male had a home-range of 76 ha. This male ranged over several ridges, slopes and valleys. A large male ranged more widely (MAP(95) of 102 ha) in flatter, more productive habitat. At the other extreme, a female with a young at foot occupied a home-range of only 14 ha.

In their preferred habitats in savanna woodlands the daily behaviour of antilopine kangaroos resembles that of the eastern grey kangaroo. During the dry season resting groups are found in shady groves of timber during the hottest part of the day. About mid-afternoon, 3–4 p.m., the first individuals or groups move out into open grassy areas to feed. At this time conditions are still hot and thermoregulatory behaviours, such as panting and forelimb licking, are seen. Within an hour after sunset all animals are grazing. What happens in the way of activity at night is undetermined but grazing continues after sunrise, with most animals foraging until about 8 a.m. With the increase of the sun's intensity groups move off to shade and by 9 a.m. almost no animals remain feeding. Antilopine kangaroo groups often return to specific camp sites. Such sites are indicated by well-used hip holes and large accumulations of faeces. Aboriginal people exploited this behaviour when hunting antilopine kangaroos.

# POPULATION STRUCTURE, DISPERSAL AND MORTALITY

The structure of a kangaroo population in a particular area may be quite different, in terms of age and sex classes, from that expected in ideal circumstances or even from similar populations in other regions. The reasons for this are different patterns of dispersal and migration, of mortality among the age and sex classes and, of course, of reproduction.

To study population structure it is necessary to be able to tell the sex and age of kangaroos in the field. Sexing of kangaroo populations is relatively easy. Males have large testes and mature males also have a distinctive body conformation. Frequently males have different colouring from that of females. The females have a pouch. But sexing of the young at foot and of juveniles is difficult in the wild. Young males that have not become sexually active have a similar build to females. Their testes are relatively small and are carried up against the body, so they may be difficult to see. Broad population surveys often have a single category for subadults of unknown sex.

Judging the age of kangaroos is difficult but not impossible. It is made feasible by two characteristics: firstly, kangaroos' teeth grow in an unusual manner (Fig. 7.3); secondly, overall body growth continues well into adulthood, especially in males (Fig. 4.2). By comparison with animals of known age timing of tooth growth can be established and correlated with measurements of body size and proportions. Consequently, the ages of kangaroos that are shot or found dead in the field can be determined to within a year or two. It also means that animals caught live can be placed in broad age categories by noting their body proportions.

# POPULATION STRUCTURE AND DYNAMICS: RED KANGAROOS

*Figure 4.1*
*Red kangaroos near Alice Springs, Central Australia, were extensively sampled between October 1959 and October 1962 and the birth-years of animals shot were determined. Several patterns emerged. The population contained many long-lived kangaroos; females made up a high proportion of these older animals. Also, recruitment to the adult population largely occurred during a few periods of sustained pasture growth. Derived from Newsome (1977).*

The structure and dynamics of red kangaroo populations have been studied more extensively than in other species because of their potential competition with sheep and cattle in our rangelands. Red kangaroo populations, as reflected in age/sex profiles, are likely to vary more than those of other species. Red kangaroos breed continuously under all but the harshest arid zone conditions, but the survival rate of young and adults varies from place to place depending on local environmental conditions. Predation from dingos or from commercial shooting also can vary markedly between districts.

In the early 1960s a study of breeding patterns and age structures in red kangaroo populations, carried out by Harry Frith and Geoff Sharman, showed considerable variability in the survival of young. In good conditions in southern New South Wales only 15 per cent of young which reached the end of their pouch life failed to survive to weaning at about one year old, while in western Queensland, which was in severe drought, 83 per cent died before weaning age. Under 'moderate' conditions (for red kangaroos) about half of the young made it to weaning. Severe droughts in the most arid parts of their range result in virtually no recruitment to the adult population. The inability of immature individuals to harvest sufficient suitable energy-rich vegetation seems to be the difficulty. Alan Newsome found from his extensive studies in central Australia that a few 'very good years' provided most of the recruitment to the adult population (Fig. 4.1).

Once a red kangaroo gets to full maturity it can cope well with the harshness of its environment. The years 1947–49 were wet years in central Australia; despite the intervening years of severe drought, in 1960 Alan Newsome found that 28 per cent of the population were over 12 years old. Information from Fowlers Gap Research Station in western New South Wales tells a similar story: studies there have indicated that much of the breeding population is even older. The extreme of longevity recorded in the field was a male aged at least

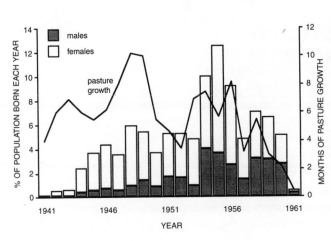

27 years when shot. This animal had been tagged in 1964 at Tero Creek in western New South Wales and it was old and in poor condition when shot in 1990 some 300 km away in South Australia.

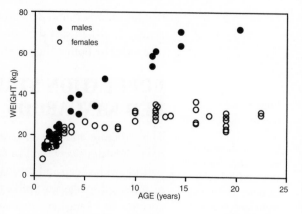

Another aspect of the population structure is sex ratio. In red kangaroos a slight male bias has been recorded at birth — the ratio of males to females was 1.05. By the time red kangaroos studied in central Australia became subadults of 2–3 years old, slightly more males had disappeared than females and the ratio was 0.82 (Fig. 4.1). At about 3–4 years old the males became sexually mature. Male mortality increased at this stage and the ratio of males to females dropped to 0.44 and stayed around this level until full maturity, when it dropped further to 0.19. This meant that in the mature population studied in Central Australia there were approximately five females for each male.

Alan Newsome suggested that this pattern in Central Australia was related to commercial shooting for skins. But this may not be the case because the sex ratio at Fowlers Gap, where shooting is rare, is similar. Shooting does have an effect on the average body size of individuals in the population. Average sizes for both sexes were smaller in the Central Australian sample than they are at Fowlers Gap. In the Central Australian study the largest male weighed 56.7 kg and the largest female was 29 kg. At Fowlers Gap large mature males generally exceed 60 kg and animals in the range 70–80 kg are not rare; peak weight seems to be reached at about 15 years old. Mature resident females are generally around 30 kg; at 10–15 years old some peak at 33–37 kg. As with males, the oldest females can lose some body condition yet still be active in breeding (Fig. 4.2).

*Figure 4.2*
*Weight change with increasing age of red kangaroos at Fowlers Gap Station in western New South Wales. The kangaroos were culled during moderate to good seasonal conditions. Derived from Edwards (1990).*

# PATTERNS OF DISPERSAL AND MIGRATION: RED KANGAROOS

Mature breeding adults of all species of kangaroos are generally sedentary, but a few adults will occasionally leave their home-ranges and move long distances, sometimes for reasons that are not clear to us. The red kangaroo has featured in our efforts to understand the stability of populations. While these dry-country kangaroos are no longer considered to be nomadic, significant movements can occur. Such movements are largely associated with the dispersal of some of the young, but adult red kangaroos may 'move camp' considerable distances. Some of these animals show fidelity to their initial area, returning to it when conditions become favourable. Other

**Figure 4.3**
*Checking the batteries of the solar-powered electric fences at Fowlers Gap Station. The electric fences enclosed two 'kangaroo-free' paddocks, of about 600 ha each, that were used in an experiment which examined competition between red kangaroos and sheep.*

individuals move away permanently, sometimes travelling hundreds of kilometres. In a Western Australian study of dispersal Tony Oliver first made allowance for capture mortality and the differential mortality of age classes. He then calculated the percentage of red kangaroos in various classes that should be found within 10 km of the capture site after 12 months. His results suggested that the majority of surviving females were sedentary, as were about a third of the adult males.

Valuable insight into the classes of red kangaroos that move beyond their usual home-ranges has come in a novel way at Fowlers Gap Research Station. For a PhD study by Glen Edwards on dietary competition between red kangaroos and sheep a 5000-volt electric fence, which pulsed once a second, was erected to exclude kangaroos from two paddocks (Fig. 4.3). These paddocks were to contain only sheep. The fence proved to be a substantial barrier to kangaroo movement, but it did 'leak'. The fence kept nearby resident kangaroos out of the paddocks once they learnt about it and avoided it. They would not go near it even if it was 'down' for a day or two because of damage or technical problems. This was not so for naive transient kangaroos which occasionally penetrated the fence even when it was live. They would start to push through and then get shocked by a pulse of electricity. Many would draw back, but some would leap forward through the fence. Once inside the fence these kangaroos avoided it and were trapped. Animals had to be culled regularly to keep the 'exclosure' paddocks relatively kangaroo-free.

After three or four months of fence operation no kangaroos that had previously been in the exclosure paddocks re-entered them. After six months the age/sex classes of animals culled showed the nature of transients in the area. In good seasonal conditions 84 per cent of the transients were subadults or young mature males. The least transient animals were old mature males. Adult females, young and old, formed about 12 per cent of the transients. Once, during a dry season in the district, there was some green feed in the area of the electric-fenced paddocks due to a localised storm. At this time a similar group of kangaroos moved into the area; 55 per cent were immature animals but, of note, the proportion of adult females involved doubled to 25 per cent of the cull. Many animals were moving through or on to the study area at this time and the population in the vicinity increased temporarily by a factor of five.

Mature red kangaroos do move home-ranges at times. Some of these are local movements, less than 10–15 km; some cover long distances. The local movements appear to be environmentally induced. The scattered thunderstorms and showers that are common in the inland lead to such movements. At Fowlers Gap Station in the warmer months such storms occur along the low ridges and footslopes of the Barrier Ranges in the western part of the Station. In dry years these storms bring forth quick-responding ephemeral grasses and herbs which provide considerable, if transient, feed. At these times some animals may temporarily move home-ranges while others may travel nightly from their usual ranges to these feeding areas. In the early morning the latter may be seen moving back to the creeklines and plains. Except in a bad drought, the increase in density of animals on these patches of green feed can generally be attributed to the movement of local animals. A similar shift in home-ranges is seen on Fowlers Gap Station when westerly winds blow in winter. Some animals move their core areas to the base of the eastern side of the ridges, presumably for protection from the cold winds. Such local movements have often been noted in other studies, such as that done by David Pridell at Kinchega National Park and the study at Mardi Station done by Tony Oliver.

Occasionally mature red kangaroos of both sexes may make long-distance movements. Something disturbs them and they are off, never to return. While it is easy to suggest reasons why such dispersion should occur, i.e. colonisation of new habitats or recolonisation of old habitats in which the residents had died out, the actual triggering factors are not known. Put simply, some individuals respond by dispersing in the face of particular social pressures, environmental stresses, or localised disturbances that do not affect other individuals. At Fowlers Gap when the electric-fenced exclosure was established a group of mature animals were displaced from their home-ranges. Most of these established new home-ranges nearby but a few left the area. Three of these were females which were subsequently resighted. The first, a young adult, was shot at McDougals Wells, some 50 km west of Fowlers Gap, about one month after relocation. The second, an older mature animal, was shot after nine months at Buckalow Station, located 250 km south of Fowlers Gap. The third, a young adult, was sighted two years later in Kinchega National Park, 150 km to the south-east of Fowlers Gap. Movements of similar magnitude have been observed in males also.

There is another type of movement which was once considered to be long-distance dispersal but is now seen in a different light: movement associated with drought. Some animals move out of their home-ranges in search of better feed. This movement is particularly noticeable if there is patchy rain elsewhere in the district.

One such event at Fowlers Gap proved to be very enlightening. David Croft and crew were engaged in a radio tracking study in early 1981 in which six adult females and four established mature males were being tracked. Their home-ranges were determined in January/February during a period of low rainfall, when vegetation was sparse. In April rain fell in a band to the north-east of the Station, starting about 25 km away. Within a week or two no radio-collared animals could be located on the Station or in its immediate vicinity, even via aerial searches. Two of the collared females were reported 25–50 km to the north-east. There was, in fact, a massive movement of animals at this time. Aerial surveys put the population of red kangaroos on the Station at 5200 in mid-February but on 20 April it had declined to 1300. Then, after general rains came through the whole district in June, the population of red kangaroos rebounded to 7500 individuals by the end of June and remained at 5700 at the end of August.

By August all the radio-collared females had returned to their original home-ranges; half had returned by the end of June. Thus there is remarkable fidelity of mature females to established home-ranges. It is likely that much of the recovery in the population of red kangaroos after the general rain was due to the return of residents as well as the movement of transients — largely immature animals and young males.

The four collared mature males did not return. One was found dead in late April (Fig. 4.4) and two were shot in August to the north-east; the other was not accounted for. But on another occasion a mature male returned to its original home-range after 25 months. Perhaps the four males would have returned, if allowed. Many of the reports of long-distance dispersal of kangaroos come from the records of professional shooters. I wonder how many of these animals might have eventually returned home. These observations suggest that kangaroos must have a much finer understanding of their environment than we have given them credit for. The mechanisms by which kangaroos sense that feed-producing rain has fallen many kilometres away and move toward it, and then eventually find their way home, are unknown. Many an evening around the campfire has been passed by field biologists discussing this problem.

Much of the knowledge of their environment may be accumulated during the wanderings of the young red kangaroos before they set up home-ranges. Little has been known about the fate of young animals. Some stay in the vicinity of their mother's home-range but most seem to disperse. It is evident from the age/sex profiles of populations that many die, especially the young males. In one of his studies in Western Australia Tony Oliver

**Figure 4.4**
*A large, radio-collared red kangaroo buck that left its home-range during a drought to seek feed associated with distant localised rain. Unlike females, few males returned to their home-ranges after general rain. However, male mortality was high and the level of potential returns is uncertain.*

radio-tracked a group of young red kangaroos despite the risk of losing the expensive collars put on the animals, which can quickly get out of the range of fixed ground tracking stations. The subadults were located from the air by flying over the district once a month in a light plane fitted with receiving aerials. It was found that most of the young animals did not completely leave the district but wandered widely within it, over distances that would include the areas of many adult home-ranges (Fig. 4.5). One male eventually did move out of the district to an area 30–40 km away; thereafter he continued his wanderings in that area. Really long-distance dispersal seemed rare.

During Tony Oliver's study a male and a female 'grew up' (Fig. 4.5). The male was about three years old when fitted with his radio collar. He maintained the movement of a subadult for a further year, wandering broadly over an area up to 10 km from the water point where he was captured. At about four years old and weighing 40 kg he settled down to a typical home-range, about 3 km in diameter. The female was initially about 16 months old and showed a wandering pattern for another 18 months. When she was almost three years old she established a tight home-range some 2 km across; six months later she was recovered and found to have a young at foot and a very small pouch young. Her initial mating had occurred before she had established a firm home-range.

**Figure 4.5**
*Changes in the pattern of movement of (A) a red kangaroo male and (B) a red kangaroo female as they mature and establish adult home-ranges in the Fortescue River region of Western Australia. Kangaroos were located monthly during the study. After Oliver (1986).*

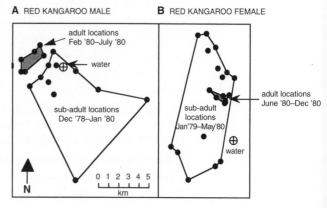

**A** RED KANGAROO MALE

adult locations Feb '80–July '80

water

sub-adult locations Dec '78–Jan '80

N

0 1 2 3 4 5
km

**B** RED KANGAROO FEMALE

adult locations June '80–Dec '80

sub-adult locations Jan'79–May'80

water

# POPULATION STRUCTURE AND MOVEMENTS OF OTHER SPECIES

## EASTERN GREY KANGAROOS

Eastern greys are sedentary and few disperse. Three of 98 animals caught and collared in the pastoral country on the northern tablelands of New South Wales by Peter Jarman and Robert Taylor dispersed beyond 10 km over several months. In Queensland observations have shown that it is common for eastern grey kangaroos to die around waterholes in drought-affected areas while good feed and water are only a few kilometres away. Among the few animals that do disperse young males predominate, but all classes, including adult females, may relocate. A small amount of radio tracking at Fowlers Gap Research Station confirms this pattern. An eastern grey female, initially with a young at foot, gradually moved her activity centre 10 km along a creek over a period of 16 months; and a subadult male moved completely off the Station in a couple of weeks, taking his expensive radio transmitter with him.

## WESTERN GREY KANGAROOS

Western greys, as with eastern greys, are generally sedentary and show strong fidelity to their home-ranges. During the Bakers Hill study in Western Australia the only animals to move regularly were sexually maturing males about five years old (45 kg). These moved, but not far; they set up new home-ranges about 1 km from their initial ranges. A small number of animals can leave an area completely and show up a considerable distance away, often in the form of an identification collar returned by an interested kangaroo shooter. A movement of 85 km by a male western grey kangaroo from Kinchega National Park in western New South Wales was uncovered in this way. The mobile proportion of the population was less than 7 per cent in the Kinchega area and about 2 per cent in Western Australia; there was no sex bias in such movements.

Not all distance movements are dispersing movements. A subadult male (27 kg) collared on Fowlers Gap Creek moved 12 km within a week to Floods Creek, an adjoining station. Two months later it returned to the site of its capture where it largely remained for the next year or so; it was seen in winter in a group with six larger males. It made at least one further excursion to Floods Creek and back, moving 18 km. This pattern has similarities to the pattern of subadult movement observed in red kangaroos in Western Australia.

## EUROS AND WALLAROOS

Past seasonal conditions, type of habitat and predation can all have significant effects on the structure of euro and wallaroo populations. The age structure of a relatively undisturbed euro population (no dingos and no

shooting) was monitored during initial
survey work at Fowlers Gap Station in
1967–68. The population contained
many long-lived individuals, including
some around 20 years old. This can be
compared with a population of eastern
wallaroos that suffered heavy hunting
(Fig. 4.6). Peaks in age groups reflect
periods of good rainfall when survival
of young was high. While there are
reports of significant mortality among
euros in times of drought, there are
also major surges in breeding when
droughts end (Fig. 2.5). Adult euros have the characteristics needed for
continued survival in their harsh environment. At Fowlers Gap, if they survive to adulthood, female euros do not show marked mortality until about
13 years of age. With males, numbers decline after the age of 6–7 years, the
age at which they put on the final growth spurt and presumably also expend
energy in starting to establish their position in the adult hierarchy.

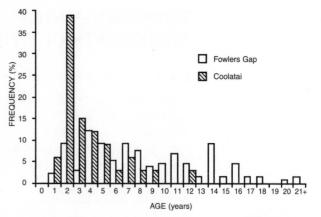

**Figure 4.6**
*Effect of harvesting
(shooting) on the
age structure of
euro/wallaroo
populations. The
Fowlers Gap euro
population was
pristine; the
population of
wallaroos at
Coolatai in
northern New
South Wales had
been heavily
harvested and had
a predominance of
young animals,
many of which had
not yet reached
breeding age. After
Russell and
Richardson (1971).*

Tim Clancy generally noted a 1:1 sex ratio at birth among euros.
However, different ratios were observed in the populations in different
parts of his study area at Fowlers Gap. The rougher terrain of the South
Ridge site was apparently a more optimum habitat and in this area of
higher euro density males were less common: the sex ratio was 0.4:1. In low
undulating country where euro densities were lower there was a greater
proportion of males. This could be explained by differential mortality or
migration of juvenile males at the two sites, or it may be due to dominant
males pushing younger males out of the major breeding areas — as has
been noted to be the case with antilopine kangaroos.

Euros are mainly sedentary but, again, some animals disperse, mainly
young males. This is indicated by work in the Pilbara and at Fowlers Gap.
The dispersal of one radio-collared young male about 2.5 years old has been
described at Fowlers Gap. After remaining in his original home-range for
over half a year, he then moved south along the hills and was 10–15 km
away when the radio-collar failed. Of four males of this age that were ear-
tagged, none was resighted again after two months. This contrasts with the
situation with females: of ten young females ear-tagged, six were known to
be in the study area six months after capture and at least four were still
there a year later. One female was observed over a four-year period and
remained and even bred in her mother's home-range.

Work done by Tim Clancy and David Croft showed that there was little
movement of euros between their two main study areas at Fowlers Gap
even though areas were only 2–4 km apart. There is evidence, though, that

euros will move to repopulate an area where numbers have been depleted through shooting. They can also move during droughts to areas where feed is available because of localised thunderstorms (Fig. 2.5). The distances and number of animals involved in these movements are not known. On the other hand, euros have been observed to stay and die in large numbers in their hilly refuges in severe droughts. Perhaps they do not move without positive incentive.

# CAUSES OF MORTALITY IN KANGAROOS

## LACK OF NUTRITION

There can be large mortality in kangaroo populations due to poor feed availability. This is especially seen in young animals after weaning and in males approaching sexual maturity. These animals do not have sufficient body reserves to cope with even small nutritional setbacks. The same applies to old animals, which may have extreme tooth wear or other age-related disabilities. Other factors also can be involved in increased mortality such as predation (at times facilitated by poor nutrition) and disease (also facilitated by poor nutrition). Significant disease mortality in particular should be seen as a multifaceted process in which an environmental stress is the initial trigger and the disease state is the terminal event.

## PREDATION

That predators impact on the lifestyle of kangaroos is obvious. The vigilance behaviour and patterns of grouping attest to this (Fig. 3.1). Habitat preferences also may be influenced. Differences in the response of grey kangaroos and red kangaroos to predation are clearly seen at Fowlers Gap Station. Driving along the floodplain of the creek in the late afternoon startles the kangaroos that have commenced to feed. The greys, both species, head straight for the creekline and the cover provided by river red gums and undergrowth of scrub. If pressed they keep to the creekline and make use of the cover and broken ground — together with their mobility — to be soon out of harm's way. Red kangaroos, on the other hand, take off away from the creek and head out into the open country. If they are forced toward the creekline they generally go straight through and out the other side. It seems that the reds are dealing with predation by getting into the open where they can rely on their superior speed.

Eagles and foxes take kangaroos and, in sheep country where dingos are excluded, they are the major predators except for humans. However, they are not a major source of kangaroo mortality. These predators generally focus on juveniles: young kangaroos often turn up in the diet of wedge-tailed eagles throughout Australia. But this is not always the case. I have seen four wedge-tailed eagles combining to hunt a mature female red kangaroo during a drought when smaller prey was scarce. Overall, in sheep country the evidence is strong that nutritional factors are primarily involved in mortality, especially as a result of drought.

## PREDATION BY DINGOS

The dog (dingo) fence, which separates the sheep country of the far north-west of New South Wales from the cattle country of Queensland and South Australia, highlights our lack of understanding of the impact of predation on kangaroos. Beyond the dog fence in the cattle country and deserts of the outback, as well as in the mountain country of eastern Australia, dingos have a major impact on kangaroo population structure. There are numerous accounts of dingos killing kangaroos and in parts of Australia kangaroos are the major food source of dingos. They are efficient predators and have most impact on the very young and the old members of each population.

The density of kangaroos 'inside' the dog fence is about 100 times the density beyond it in the dingo country. It is easy to say that this difference is simply a matter of predation, but the dingo country is also largely cattle country. The vegetation is different, particularly the tree density, due to the different grazing patterns occurring over the last 100 years. It may be that lower feed and/or water availability for kangaroos in the cattle country contributes to their limited numbers. From his work in Sturt National Park, Martin Denny pointed out that the dingo fence also stops natural immigration from New South Wales into the 'corner' of Queensland and South Australia. If kangaroo numbers are reduced by drought, disease or predation in the 'corner' cattle country, then their numbers could easily be kept low by continued predation by dingos.

The level of predation by dingos on kangaroos is related to the pattern of prey availability. Where there are rabbits these are the preferred prey of the dingo. The changing patterns in dingo prey have been shown in a long-term study carried out through good seasons and drought near Alice Springs in central Australia. In good seasons rabbits and small rodents, which were common, made up over 80 per cent of the prey and red kangaroos were generally not taken. With the onset of drought and the decline of the previous prey, red kangaroos came to make up about one-third of the diet, even when they were

**Figure 4.7**
*Effect of drought on the prey eaten by dingos in Central Australia: (A) relative weights of available prey in a good season and in a drought; (B) proportions by weight of prey in the stomachs of dingos at those times. In drought kangaroos became a substantial item despite very low availability. After Corbett and Newsome (1987).*

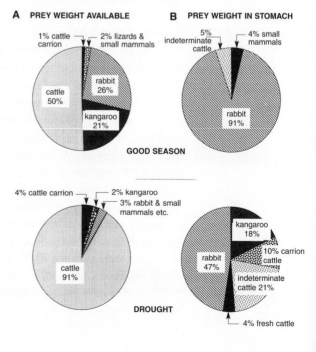

uncommon (Fig. 4.7). Kangaroo numbers did not increase after the drought if the dingos were able to maintain their numbers by eating cattle carrion. On the Nullarbor Plain, where small rodents are less abundant, dingos primarily took rabbits and red kangaroos in a ratio of about 2:1, as indicated in another study by gut content analysis.

In the Fortescue River region of northern Western Australia, rabbits are absent and small terrestrial mammals are not common. Red kangaroos and euros were found to be the predominant prey of dingos in this tropical semi-desert region. In this area Peter Thomson of the Department of Conservation and Land Management noted that dingos seemed to specialise in large prey: calves were also attacked at times. Associated with this hunting of large prey was a higher degree of dingo sociality than seen elsewhere. Dingos cooperating in groups were more successful than solitary dingos in hunting such prey. Thomson found that only 5 per cent of chases by solitary dingos were successful in catching a kangaroo and even then about two-thirds of these kangaroos eventually escaped. In pack hunting 13 per cent of chases were successful in catching the kangaroo; only a quarter of these kangaroos managed in the end to get away. Kangaroos were hunted even when easy-to-obtain cattle carrion was available. Thomson found that at times dingos reduced the kangaroo population to the dingos' own detriment — such that there was a decline in the dingos' population size and a breakdown of their social structure.

A dingo has difficulty in catching a fit adult kangaroo, but some age groups of kangaroos appear to be particularly vulnerable to dingos. The pattern of kills on the Fortescue River is shown in Fig. 4.8. These data are for euros, which were more abundant than red kangaroos, but kills of red kangaroos showed a similar trend. Old males were the main group killed. Old females were the next most susceptible group, followed by immature and young adults. In other circumstances the relative number of young killed may be much higher. In Sturt National Park in the north-west corner of New South Wales dingos established themselves after damage to the dog fence caused by flooding. The dingos ambushed red kangaroos as they came in to water and 83 individuals were killed in a few weeks. Juveniles made up 80 of these kills. Excess killing, apparently surplus to needs as in this case, has often been reported. A dingo kills a kangaroo mainly by bites to the head and neck; bites to the legs and tail are also common but these are aimed at knocking the kangaroo over in order to stop it.

**Figure 4.8**
*Ages of euros killed by dingos in the Fortescue River region of Western Australia compared with the age structure of the general population in a nearby district. Dingos preferentially take young animals and old males. After Oliver (1986).*

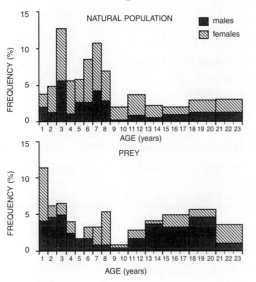

## PAST PREDATORS

It is obvious that kangaroos have evolved in association with predators. The dingo has been in Australia for only 4000 years, so other predators must have influenced patterns of kangaroo behaviour. The dingo-sized thylacine or Tasmanian wolf, *Thylacinus cynocephalus*, was replaced on the mainland by the dingo as the main large generalist predator. In morphology the thylacine is remarkably convergent on the wolf and apparently it hunted like the wolf. Eye-witness accounts tell us that the thylacine hunted by active pursuit. Going back into the fossil history there is evidence for a range of thylacinid hunters, from small fox-sized forms to species larger than the Tasmanian wolf.

Other notable predators would have included the marsupial 'lion', *Thylacoleo carnifex*. These leopard-like marsupials existed during the Pleistocene period until about 30,000 years ago, in association with the large kangaroos and cow-sized diprotodontids. The disappearance of these large marsupials, the 'megafauna', happened at approximately the same time as the arrival of that other extremely potent predator, man. The impact of Aborigines, perhaps combined with the effects of the last glaciation, had a devastating effect on the large macropodids. All the giant browsing forms succumbed but the swift medium-sized kangaroos survived. These are now our largest kangaroos. Australia was also the home of a giant goanna, *Megalania prisca* (Fig. 9.1), which was twice the body length of the largest living lizard, the Komodo dragon. Given the ability of the Komodo dragon to catch and kill goats and deer from ambush, it would seem that kangaroos might well have had cause for alarm when *Megalania prisca* was around. Pythons up to 6 m in length were also part of the Pleistocene megafauna; these too may have been predators on kangaroos.

## DISEASE

Since 1980 records have been kept of health inspections of kangaroo carcases processed for export as game meat for human consumption. Of over 200,000 red, eastern grey and western grey carcases less than 0.7 per cent were found to have some form of pathological condition. Such a figure is considerably better than that for domestic animals slaughtered at export or domestic abattoirs. Most of the rejected kangaroo carcases were infected with the filarioid nematode worm, *Pelecitus roemeri*, which is usually found in the connective tissue under the skin, often around the pelvis or knees. It is a relatively benign organism. This means that there is little obvious disease in kangaroo populations. Disease outbreaks do occur but the infected animals may not live long.

Significant disease outbreaks which cause population 'crashes' often are associated with some form of stress such as extreme environmental conditions, e.g. drought, flooding or severe wet and cold weather. In this case the

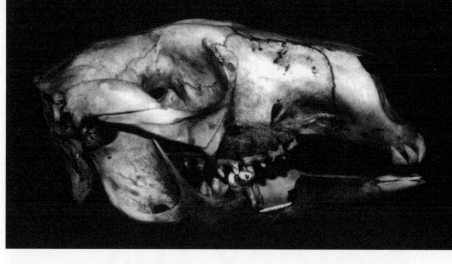

**Figure 4.9**
*Skull of a red kangaroo showing the erosion of the lower jaw associated with the chronic disease 'lumpy jaw'. The jaw finally broke and presumably led to the death of the kangaroo.*

disease may be only the 'terminal cause' of death. The diseases of kangaroos have been reviewed by Speare and co-workers and they make this point clearly. Diseases are best viewed as an endpoint, an aspect of death rate which must be understood in order to gain an accurate view of population dynamics. For example, a kangaroo may have died from septicaemia, but it might as well be considered to have died from the lumpy jaw that gave rise to the septicaemia. Lumpy jaw is a chronic jaw infection due to the bacterium *Fusobacterium necrophorum* (Fig. 4.9). And from this standpoint consideration has to be given to the drought that set the conditions for acquiring the lumpy jaw, and to the degradation of habitat that made the region more subject to the decreased rainfall. Generally, major diseases in wild animals should be treated as multilayered processes.

An example of this complexity was reported by Renata Jaremovic. She noted the die-off of large numbers of subadult eastern grey kangaroos during one winter in the southern highlands of New South Wales. The terminal cause of death was pneumonia, but this was stress-related and associated with a dry autumn and poor pasture growth followed by abnormally cold and wet conditions in winter. The bulk of the animals that died were about the age of weaning. Some old males also died at that time and many females lost their pouch young. The actual pathology of the death of pouch young is unknown. It is suspected that the nutritional stress associated with lower milk production leads to lowered immune responses and predisposition to disease, particularly of the gut.

Epidemic mortality does occur at times; the cause is not always understood. Such events are often associated with a degree of environmental stress, but not always. One event occurred in western Queensland in June–August 1983. All species of kangaroo in the area were affected. They died in good condition and showed no gross pathological changes. A variety of causes have been suggested for this epidemic, ranging from mosquito-spread viral disease to the kangaroos being 'worried' to death by swarms of black flies (*Austrosimulium pestilens*). But these are only speculations and the actual reasons for the deaths are unknown.

# CHAPTER

# REPRODUCTIVE BIOLOGY AND BEHAVIOUR

## INTRODUCTION

The delightful picture of a doe kangaroo with a large joey looking out of her pouch is one of the evocative things that characterise Australian marsupials. Having a young spend much of its early development in a pouch instead of within the body frequently evokes the question: why are the marsupials so different in their reproduction? Does it represent a stagnation in evolutionary progress or is it just an alternative (and perhaps even better) reproductive strategy to that used by the placentals? The former view prevailed for many years but is now being challenged, principally from an ecological viewpoint. The question now appears to be: why have the *placentals* diverged from the basic pattern of vertebrate reproduction? The hormonal and structural basis on which the live-bearing of young (viviparity) developed in marsupials and placentals was certainly established in monotremes and probably evolved even before the emergence of reptiles. The shelled egg of the reptiles, which is still seen in birds, provided the basic structures used in the development of viviparity.

Despite the attention given to the evolution of viviparity, the most important feature of mammalian reproduction was actually the evolution of milk feeding. Lactation and maternal care are at the base of mammalian evolution. Remember that the monotremes lay eggs but nurse their young. Monotremes are an earlier offshoot of the lineage that gave rise to the marsupials and placentals. Once lactation was established it opened the door to an extended period of parental care and its benefits. The placentals achieved this by combining lactation with an extension of intrauterine development. The marsupials, on the other hand, extended extrauterine development and placed more reliance on lactation than on nourishment of the embryo via the placenta.

Hugh Tyndale-Biscoe and Marilyn Renfree, in their excellent book on reproduction in marsupials, conclude that viviparity evolved in the common ancestor of the marsupials and placentals, after the line to the monotremes had diverged. This occurred possibly in the early Cretaceous period, more than 100 million years ago. Viviparity evolved when ancestral mammals were tiny insectivores. It is plausible that these mammals gave birth to many very immature young and had several litters a year. These young may have been kept in a nest, not a pouch. The differences in reproductive anatomy between the marsupials and placentals, notably in the female urogenital system, probably occurred after the evolution of viviparity. Early in their divergence the difference in reproduction between the two groups of small insectivorous mammals would have been hard to discern, as is still the case with some small marsupial and placental species.

An increase in body size of some lineages of marsupials and placentals has accentuated reproductive differences. Adult body size has a marked impact on reproductive patterns and life history strategies. An increase in brain size may be the primary selective advantage in the evolution of large size. However, whatever the benefits, larger size is associated with increased gestation length, reduced litter size, slower growth rates and increased life span. The kangaroos fit into this pattern.

The placentals adapted to increasing size by extending gestation and giving birth to relatively advanced young. The longer gestation has involved an extension of the function of the placenta. The development of the young of kangaroos has been supported by a longer period of lactation. The extended period of growth and development is carried out in a much enlarged pouch. Such a pattern would seem a simpler solution than extending uterine accommodation. However, it should also be pointed out that the reproductive patterns of kangaroos are not 'typical' marsupial patterns, but are highly derived.

# REPRODUCTIVE ANATOMY — FEMALE MARSUPIALS

Before discussing reproduction in kangaroos we need some background information on marsupials generally.

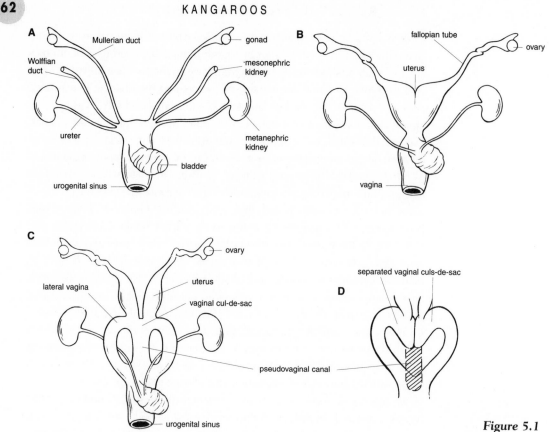

**A**

Mullerian duct

gonad

Wolffian duct

mesonephric kidney

ureter

metanephric kidney

bladder

urogenital sinus

**B**

fallopian tube

ovary

uterus

vagina

**C**

ovary

lateral vagina

uterus

vaginal cul-de-sac

pseudovaginal canal

urogenital sinus

**D**

separated vaginal culs-de-sac

pseudovaginal canal

*Figure 5.1*
*Development of the female reproductive system in marsupials and placentals: (A) early sexually undifferentiated stage; (B) basic placental system; (C) marsupial system, kangaroo form with fused vaginal culs-de-sac and open pseudovaginal canal; (D) marsupial condition seen in the dasyurids with separated vaginal culs-de-sac and a pseudovaginal canal which is open only at parturition. After Dawson (1983).*

In the embryos of amniote vertebrates (reptiles, birds and mammals) there are three pairs of ducts which are concerned with excretion and reproduction. These are the Wolffian ducts, the ureters and the Mullerian ducts or oviducts (Fig 5.1). The Wolffian ducts are initially involved with excretion but during development become sperm ducts or the vasa deferentia of the adult. The Mullerian ducts provide the fallopian tubes, uterus and vagina of the female tract. During development in marsupials the ureters pass to the bladder between the Mullerian ducts, whereas in placentals the ureters enter the bladder by passing lateral to, or outside, the Mullerian ducts.

Tyndale-Biscoe and Renfree consider that the independent reorganisation of the urogenital ducts in early marsupials and placentals was related to a separation of the urogenital tract and the gut and not primarily related to reproduction. I agree; the reorganisation probably occurred so that the ureters would open directly into the bladder, instead of the lower gut. If the urine is held in an impermeable bladder, as distinct from the permeable lower gut, it can be concentrated, thus enabling a considerable saving of water when excreting waste products from the kidney.

Previously, it had been suggested that placentals had a selective change in embryogenesis which resulted in the alternative path for the ureters. This change, it was suggested, allowed for the fusion of the Mullerian duct derivatives to form a large uterus and vagina and thus permit the production of a large advanced young. Such a simple explanation for the reproductive differences between placentals and marsupials is not supportable. Fusion of the Mullerian ducts to give a large uterus is not necessary to achieve a large young. Some placentals, even ungulates which give birth to advanced young, have completely separate uterine horns and marsupials also show some fusion and development of the reproductive tract.

In marsupials there are two lateral vaginae up which the sperm travels on insemination. In all ancestral mammalian forms birth or egg laying presumably occurred via these lateral vaginae, the homologues of the midline vagina of placentals. In modern marsupials, such as kangaroos, birth occurs through a midline pseudovaginal canal. This short cut to the outside forms from the cul-de-sac formed where each lateral vagina loops around a ureter at the base of the uteri (Fig. 5.1). A more ancestral vaginal condition is still found in small dasyurids and some didelphids, where there is still a septum separating right and left vaginal culs-de-sac (Fig. 5.1). In most marsupials the pseudovaginal canal opens and closes with each birth.

The urogenital tract of kangaroos (Fig. 5.1) is basically similar to that of other marsupials. The ovary, which produces the eggs, is enclosed by the delicate and membraneous fimbria. The fimbria is an extension of the funnel or infundibulum of the oviduct into which the eggs are shed. These pass into an expanded region, the ampulla, where fertilisation most likely occurs. The ampulla leads into a very convoluted section of the oviduct, the isthmus, which in turn leads into the uterus. At the junction of the oviduct and uterus there is a constriction or sphincter that allows the passage of the egg but normally prevents backflow of fluid from the uterus.

There are two discrete uteri. They have two basic layers: the internal glandular endometrium, which can produce copious secretions, and the outer myometrium. The myometrium is made up of layers of muscle whose function is to expel the young at the appropriate time. The reproductive cycle results in major variations in the form and function of the tissues in the uteri. With kangaroos the uteri have separate openings into a combined vaginal cul-de-sac. The lateral and median vaginae join at the beginning of the urogenital sinus, into which the urethra from the bladder also empties. Among the kangaroos the epithelia of the large vaginal cul-de-sac and the urogenital sinus become continuous at the time of the first birth. A permanent median vagina is thus formed (except in the eastern grey kangaroo). In view of this condition it is difficult to accept that simple anatomical constraints would have limited the size of marsupial young if there had been strong adaptive pressures for the birth of large young.

# FEMALE MARSUPIAL REPRODUCTIVE CYCLES

## THE GENERAL MARSUPIAL PATTERN

A feature of the gestation period of marsupials is its short duration. The foetal marsupial may spend as little as 12–13 days in the reproductive tract. Why is the gestation period so short and what happens in this time?

In female birds and mammals the reproductive tract has two primary functions. The first is the reception and transport of spermatozoa to the egg so that fertilisation can occur. The second function is to provide the egg with coats and 'shells' and to provide nourishment for the developing embryo. The complex sequence of events which make this possible is called the oestrus cycle. There are two phases of the cycle: the pro-oestrus or follicular phase and the luteal or secretory phase. These names refer to the stages which occur in the activity of the ovary during the cycle, but are reflected in the whole reproductive tract.

The broad sequence of changes in the ovaries and genital tract are similar in most marsupials (Fig. 5.2). The breeding cycle starts with the pro-oestrus phase, during which the ovaries enlarge and egg-containing follicles grow and mature. Cell division and growth of the uterine epithelium and secretory glands occur at this time. The vaginal regions also increase in size and secretory activity to enable the reception and transport of seminal fluid. These initial changes are controlled by increased levels of oestrogen produced in the ovary by the cells of the growing follicles. These oestrogen-induced changes reach their peak about the time of oestrus or 'heat'; the female is then receptive to males and copulation may occur. Ovulation, the bursting of the ovarian follicles and the shedding of eggs, occurs 1–2 days after oestrus. Growth of the uterine glands continues at this time and for a further short period. The epithelium of the vaginal area regresses, its job of transporting and storing spermatozoa being finished.

**Figure 5.2**
*Profiles of plasma progesterone during oestrus cycles with pregnancy in (A) brushtail possums (a general marsupial pattern) and (B) tammar wallabies (kangaroos appear similar). Features of the macropodine pattern (B) are the early progesterone peak around days 5–6, the extension associated with gestation occupying almost all the cycle, and the dramatic fall at birth. Also shown (B) are plasma oestrogen (oestradiol) levels through the cycle. Two significant rises occur, one at days 5–6, coincident with the progesterone peak, and one just after birth that is associated with ovulation and oestrus. Derived from Tyndale-Biscoe and Renfree (1987).*

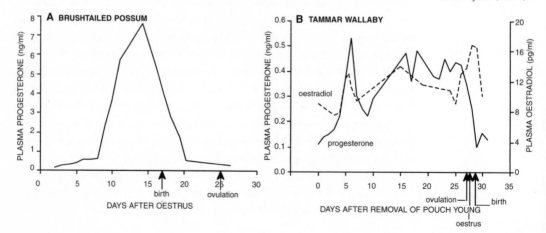

The brief post-oestrus proliferative phase in the uterus is followed by a secretory or luteal phase, which is under the control of the hormone progesterone which is produced by the corpus luteum. The corpus luteum is a gland that forms from the wall of the ruptured ovarian follicle. During the luteal phase the uteri become highly secretory and swollen and more vascular. Abundant secretory material is poured into the uterine lumen to provide nutrients for the growth of the embryo and its associated membranes. The luteal phase varies in length in different marsupials and is followed by a regressive phase during which there is a reduction in size, complexity and secretory activity of the uterine glands. Anoestrus, an overall shutdown of the system, follows in those species that have only one oestrus per breeding season. However, in continuous breeders or species that have more than one oestrus the regressive or post-luteal phase grades into the next pro-oestrus phase.

Insemination and a resulting pregnancy do not interrupt the oestrus cycle of marsupials as they do in placentals. This is a significant feature of marsupial reproduction. Pregnancy does not inhibit the continuation of the oestrus cycle, but lactation does, the ovarian inhibition being mediated by the suckling stimulus. If continued lactation is prevented by the removal of the young soon after birth the next oestrus occurs when expected. In many marsupials gestation does not last past the luteal phase, but the situation is variable, notably in kangaroos.

## THE KANGAROO REPRODUCTIVE CYCLE

The reproductive cycle of kangaroos and their relatives differs from the basic marsupial pattern in that gestation is extended from about half the oestrus cycle to occupy almost all of it (Fig. 5.2). The embryo in a kangaroo is maintained in the uterus well into the next pro-oestrus phase, with birth occurring only a day or two before the next oestrus and mating (Table 5.1).

The relatively longer gestation period of kangaroos is associated with a lengthening of the secretory phase in the uteri via the corpus luteum. The aim of this longer gestation is to produce a young at birth that is larger and more advanced. This may seem surprising, given its very small size at birth, but the newborn kangaroo is relatively bigger and more developed than non-macropodoid marsupials. Leon Hughes and co-workers have shown this increased development to have significance in the journey of the newborn to the pouch and its attachment to a teat. The more advanced state, particularly in neurological organisation, means that the investment in the single young is less likely to go astray.

An unusual feature of reproduction in kangaroos and wallabies is embryonic diapause. During diapause a viable embryo is carried in the uterus for long periods (many months) with its development arrested at the stage of a blastocyst, which consists of some 70–100 cells and is only about 0.25 mm in diameter. Because of the extension of the gestation period into the pro-oestrus phase of the next ovulation, mating and fertilisation can occur a day or two after the birth. (The grey kangaroos are an exception to this pattern, with the western grey kangaroo not showing diapause at all.) The embryo produced following this post-partum mating will not successfully develop past the blastocyst stage until a specific signal is given. If a young has not taken up residence in the pouch and started to nurse there is a specific pulse of progesterone secretion about six days after the birth (Fig. 5.2). This pulse is necessary if the blastocyst is to continue development. If there is a young suckling in the pouch then lactation inhibits the corpus luteum via the hormone prolactin. The corpus luteum then becomes quiescent and no pulse of progesterone occurs and the blastocyst enters diapause. It will only recommence development when the lactational inhibition is removed, either by loss of the pouch young or by the reduced lactation toward the end of pouch life.

The general timing of events in the reproductive cycles of kangaroos is basically similar for all species (Table 5.1), but the grey kangaroos do differ in some details from the red kangaroos and the 'robustus' group of walla-roos. There are also differences in timing among the subspecies of the wal-laroos; limited data also suggest that the antilopine kangaroo may have a longer cycle than the red kangaroo.

### Table 5.1
Timing and basic features of the reproductive cycles of kangaroos(a)

| Species | Oestrus cycle, days | Gestation, days | Post-partum mating | Blastocyst diapause | Loss of PY to next birth, days |
|---------|---------------------|-----------------|--------------------|---------------------|--------------------------------|
| Red | 34.8±0.6 | 33.2±0.2 | yes | yes | 34.7±0.3 |
| Wallaroo | 33.6±0.6 | 32.7±1.5 | yes | yes | 30.9±2.0 |
| Euro | 36.7±3.5(b) | 33.4±1.5 | yes | yes | 34.9±3.2 |
| Antilopine | 41.0±4.2(c) | 33.9±1.3 | no | ? | ? |
| East. grey | 45.6±9.8(d) | 36.4±1.6 | no | yes(e) | 28–32 |
| West. grey | 34.9±4.4 | 30.6±2.6 | no | no | never |

(a) Values are means ± standard deviation.

(b) Cycle length from oestrus to post-partum oestrus. Without a birth the cycle may be longer.

(c) Length of cycle without birth.

(d) Median value is 42 days. Longer cycles may be due to the effects of seasonal anoestrus.

(e) Diapause is uncommon and not the result of a post-partum mating.

**Plate 1**

*Fowlers Gap Station, the University of New South Wales' arid zone research station in the dry rangelands of far western New South Wales. Variation in landform, from the rocky hills down to the tree-covered creeks and out to the wide, open plains, provides habitat for four species of kangaroo. Euros are in the hills, eastern and western grey kangaroos are near the creeks and red kangaroos are on the plains.*

**Plate 2**

*Eastern grey kangaroos, Macropus giganteus, male and female, from eastern New South Wales.*

**Plate 3**
*Female western
grey kangaroo,
Macropus
fuliginosus, from
western New South
Wales.*

**Plate 4**
*Male red kangaroo,
Macropus rufus,
hopping across the
plains of Fowlers
Gap Station, far
western New
South Wales.*

**Plate 5**
*Red kangaroos with the red and blue extremes of coat colour. Males are usually red, but among both sexes all colours and shades can be found.*

**Plate 6**
*Male eastern wallaroo, Macropus robustus robustus, from eastern New South Wales. Females are distinctly smaller and lighter in colour.*

**Plate 7**
*Male euro,
Macropus robustus
erubescens, from
Tibooburra, far
western New South
Wales. Its rusty
brown colour is
characteristic of the
males from central
and western
Australia. The
northern wallaroo is
similar.*

**Plate 8**
*Female euro from
the hills of Fowlers
Gap Station. The
females are slighter
in build and usually
lighter in colour
than the males.*

**Plate 9**
*Male black wallaroo,
Macropus bernardus, from
the Arnhem Land region of
northern Australia
(photo David Croft).*

**Plate 10**
*Antilopine kangaroos,
Macropus antilopinus, male
and female, from the
Northern Territory. These are
the most social of kangaroos.
The male has a characteristic
enlargement of the nasal
region, possibly related
to increased demands for
evaporative cooling in the
tropical environment.*

**Plate 11**
A cannon net set up at a sheep watering trough to catch kangaroos for the fitting of radio collars. The kangaroos are male and female western greys.

**Plate 12**
A male eastern grey kangaroo courting an oestrus female. He is following her closely and stroking her tail.

**Plate 13**
Copulation of euros. The male is 'Boss': a particularly large, aggressive and successful buck from the Fowlers Gap hills (photo David Croft).

**Plate 14**
An early pouch young (about two weeks old) of a western grey kangaroo. At this stage the tiny joey is permanently attached to a nipple and its presence is largely ignored by the mother, except for pouch cleaning.

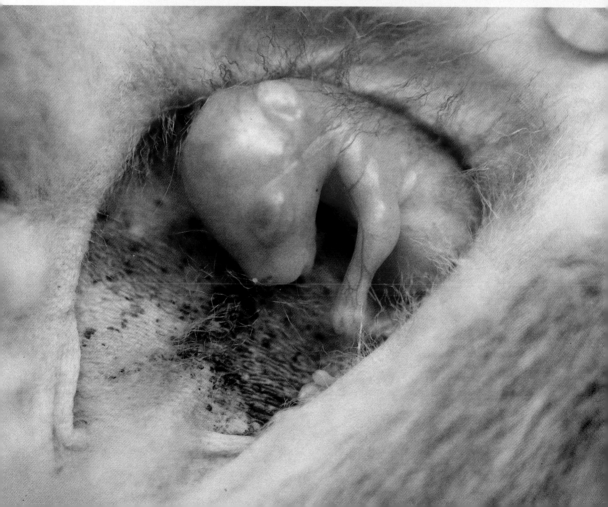

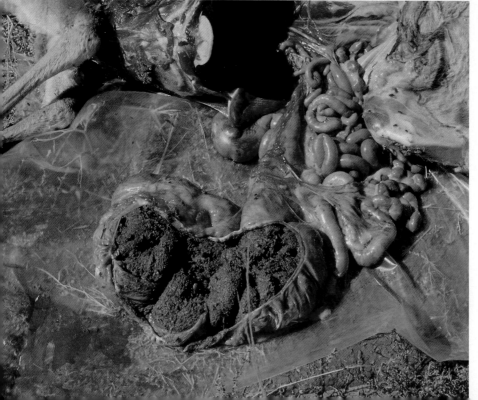

**Plate 15**
A young kangaroo initially gets to know the outside world from the comfort and safety of its mother's pouch. Intake of herbage can be high before the joey leaves the pouch (photo Mark Chappell).

**Plate 16**
A dissection of the gut of a red kangaroo, showing the large, tubiform foregut which is largely filled with green grass.

With red kangaroos, euros and wallaroos breeding is continuous under good conditions. The oestrus cycles are about 35 days, 1–3 days longer than the gestation (pregnancy) period. There is a post-birth oestrus with mating 1–3 days after the birth. The embryo resulting from this mating enters embryonic diapause if the recently born young has succeeded in reaching the pouch and attaching to a teat. The length of pregnancy after loss of a pouch young and reactivation of the dormant blastocyst is 30–40 days, the longer periods being associated with a greater intensity of suckling from a young at foot. If the female is not carrying a dormant blastocyst the time from loss of the pouch young to next oestrus will be about 32 days, but Bill Poole and Jim Merchant of CSIRO found that the variation is large. In the usual course of events the young from the blastocyst is born within a day of the permanent pouch exit of the previous young.

The grey kangaroos can breed at any time of the year but they are usually seasonal breeders. Oestrus and births generally occur during September to March with the peak activity occurring in late spring and early summer. The eastern grey has a more variable breeding pattern than the western grey, especially in the northern parts of its range. Grey kangaroos differ from red kangaroos and the wallaroo group in that gestation takes less of the oestrus cycle, especially in the eastern grey where the pregnancy period may be some ten days shorter than the oestrus cycle.

Diapausing blastocysts are rare in eastern grey kangaroos and function differently from the pattern seen in red kangaroos and the wallaroo group. Immediate post-birth oestrus does not occur. Under favourable conditions a female will mate when the pouch young is about six months old, with the resulting embryo remaining quiescent due to lactational inhibition. Again the stage of arrested development is that of the 70–100 cell unilaminar blastocyst. The embryo recommences development to be born immediately after final pouch exit by the previous young, at ten months of age, or if the pouch young is prematurely lost. In western grey kangaroos diapausing blastocysts do not occur. Bill Poole and Peter Catling noted two unusual cases during their extensive studies on western grey kangaroos. In these cases the female mated while carrying a pouch young and the pregnancy proceeded to birth without quiescence. The resulting young failed to survive in the pouch with the older sibling.

# EGGS AND EGG MEMBRANES

In the adaptation to life on land the evolution of the cleidoic or enclosed egg was a major development. It freed the vertebrates, from the reptiles onward, from the need to return to water to lay eggs. It also provided sufficient resources for the young to become more or less independent at hatching. The basic feature of the developing cleidoic egg is a series of compartments:

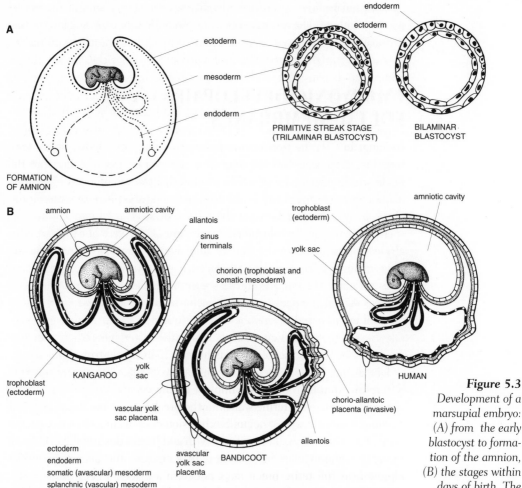

**Figure 5.3**
*Development of a marsupial embryo: (A) from the early blastocyst to formation of the amnion, (B) the stages within days of birth. The arrangements of foetal membranes are shown for a simple yolk sac placenta, as in kangaroos, and an invasive chorio-allantoic placenta combined with yolk sac placenta, as in bandicoots. The placental condition, with only an invasive chorio-allantoic placenta, as in humans, is also shown. After Dawson (1983).*

amnion, yolk sac and allantois (Fig. 5.3). The amnion grows over the embryo and encloses it in a fluid-filled cushioning sac. The yolk sac is an outgrowth of the embryonic gut and encloses the yolk, while another outgrowth, the allantois, stores metabolic waste products. Both the yolk sac and the allantois can become partly vascularised and involved in the exchange of respiratory gases. In viviparous mammals the yolk sac and/or the allantois become placentae and involved in exchange of nutrients between the foetus and the mother.

The eggs of kangaroos (and other marsupials) have a full set of shell membranes, as found in reptiles and birds, but they are much reduced. The yolk is also greatly reduced resulting in very small eggs, only about 0.12 mm in diameter. The eggs of placentals tend to be smaller still, although they overlap the marsupial range. In kangaroos the shell membranes, including the outer tertiary membrane of keratinous protein, persist for much of pregnancy, rupturing only in the last third of the gestation period. Placentals have eliminated the outer shell membrane. The significance of the persistent shell membranes in marsupials is undecided, but the suggestion that it provides a necessary immunoprotective barrier separating foetal tissues from maternal tissues is now not accepted.

# EMBRYONIC DEVELOPMENT AND FOETAL MEMBRANES

In kangaroos fertilisation occurs before the outer keratinous shell membrane is formed around the egg. The egg is shed into the fibria of the oviduct covered only with the thin secondary shell membrane, the zona pellucida. Spermatozoa attach to the zona pellucida and proceed to dissolve it. Once one succeeds and effects fertilisation there is an inhibition of further sperm penetration, possibly involving the initial secretion of a mucoid coat.

Development within the mother requires mechanisms for nutrient and gas exchange. In marsupials and placentals the yolk sac and allantois have been variously adapted to provide the embryo's needs. When foetal membranes, such as the embryonic yolk sac or allantois, are applied to the uterine wall the structure formed is referred to as a placenta.

In kangaroos and many other marsupials the yolk sac is primarily involved and a 'yolk sac' placenta is formed. This facilitates respiratory gas exchange and provides the developing embryo in the uterus with nutrients which are additional to those supplied by the egg yolk. The yolk sac placenta adheres to the uterine wall after the breakdown of the outer shell, but fusion of tissues does not occur. Such fusion does occur in bandicoots and placentals, where the allantois fuses with and breaks down the uterine wall to form a chorio-allantoic placenta. In kangaroos the allantois expands rapidly near full term, but it does not form a placenta because it is prevented from doing so by the expanded vascularised yolk sac (Fig 5.3). There are indications that in kangaroos' yolk sac placentae there is a division of function. The vascular part of the yolk sac placenta seems to be largely involved in respiratory gas exchange; it expands rapidly in the later stages of gestation when the metabolic rate of the foetus also rises. The non-vascular part of the yolk sac is concerned with the transfer of nutrients and the building blocks for growth, such as proteins.

# BIRTH AND THE CLIMB TO THE POUCH

Parturition is not a trivial event even though the young is so small. In fact *because* it is so small and fragile it is important that the mother acts to give the tiny young the best possible chance of reaching the pouch and attaching to a teat. She does this largely through pouch cleaning and birth posture. Although there was early evidence of an unaided climb to the pouch by the newborn joey, it was not until the observations of Geoff Sharman and John Calaby in 1964 that the process was fully described in the red kangaroo. Our understanding of the process of birth has been expanded by the work of Hugh Tyndale-Biscoe and Marilyn Renfree and their co-workers on the tammar wallaby, which appears to follow the pattern seen in kangaroos.

One of the signs that birth is approaching is pouch cleaning. The pouch skin secretes a waxy compound which dries to a dark scale if the pouch has been unoccupied. The female kangaroo holds the pouch open with her forepaws and sticks her head well into it and licks the scale away. Cleaning begins 1–2 days before birth; it is most intensive 1–2 hours before birth, though by then the pouch is clean. Licking of the urogenital opening also increases in intensity near birth.

In this intensive phase the female adopts a birth position which is characteristic for each species of kangaroo. With the red kangaroo the tail is passed between the legs, the legs are extended forward and the pelvis is rotated forward. The mother usually supports herself with her back against a tree or shrub; her weight is on her lower back. Wallaroo group and

**Figure 5.4**
*Birth position of an eastern grey kangaroo. The female has been cleaning the inside of the pouch just before giving birth. Some of her weight is still on the hind legs; at later stages the legs are pushed forward and the full weight is taken on the tail.*

antilopine females adopt a similar position, except that the antilopine does not appear to support her back against a vertical object. The birth posture is a little different in the grey kangaroos, according to Bill Poole. When they squat readying for the birth they do not bring their tail forward between their legs but keep it in the normal position (Fig. 5.4). The pelvis is twisted forward advancing the cloaca closer to the pouch. The legs are thrust forward with the toes off the ground, the weight being taken by the heels.

Just before birth the small yellow yolk sac appears at the urogenital opening; following this comes the clear allantois. Within seconds birth occurs, with the foetus still enclosed in the amnion. The newborn remains still for only 10–15 seconds before beginning to tear its way out of the amnion and start its climb to the pouch. The young climbs through the fur with a swimming motion using alternate forelegs. The umbilical cord breaks after about 3 cm of the climb. The time taken for the young to disappear over the edge of the pouch is about three minutes.

The mother takes no obvious active role in the process apart from ensuring that she maintains the proper position and cleans up the area. Once the newborn reaches the rim of the pouch it climbs down to the nipples and attaches within a few minutes. The young at this stage has a sense of direction, i.e. up and down, that is determined by the inner ear which is advanced in its development. The sense of smell is also functional at this stage and the young appears to be able to distinguish certain structures by touch. It is by these means that it is able to rapidly find and attach to the nipple.

## ANATOMY AND PHYSIOLOGY — MALES

Externally, the feature of reproductive anatomy of male kangaroos that distinguishes them from most placentals is the positioning of the penis behind the testes. When relaxed the penis is S-shaped in structure and enclosed in a preputial sac formed by an invagination of the skin at the base of the cloaca. When erect during sexual arousal it is extended downward and forward by eversion of the sac through the cloaca.

The paired testes and epididymides are located in the pendulous scrotum. The surface of the scrotum is lightly furred and the skin has a large number of sweat glands. These characteristics, together with the counter-current arrangement of the blood supply to the scrotum, assist in temperature regulation of the scrotum. It is essential for normal functioning that the testes be kept several (2–5) degrees cooler than body temperature. The reason for this is not clear. A strong cremaster muscle surrounds the spermatic cord and holds the scrotum tight against the body wall during cold weather and in times of stress. In warm conditions and after strenuous activity the muscle is relaxed and the scrotum hangs well away from the body wall.

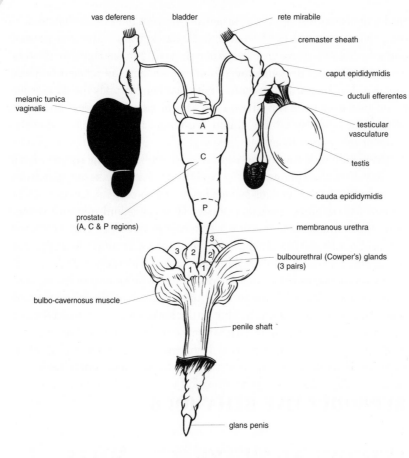

**Figure 5.5**
*The basic
structures of the
reproductive system
of a male
macropodine (a
tammar wallaby).
The left testis and
epididymis are
shown still enclosed
in the melanin-
darkened tunica
vaginalis, with
the tail of the
epididymis forming
a distinct bulge. On
the right the tunica
vaginalis has been
removed to show
the structure and
relationships of
the testis, ductuli
efferentes,
epididymis and vas
deferens. The
carrot-shaped
prostate
is connected to the
penile urethra by a
membranous
urethral segment.
After Hume et al.
(1989).*

The overall reproductive tract of male kangaroos is shown in Fig. 5.5 which comes, together with much of the information about males, from a recent review by Russell Jones of Newcastle University. The basic structure in kangaroos is similar to that of placentals but there are differences, especially with the accessory glands. The testes of kangaroos are ovoid. Spermatogenesis occurs in the convoluted semeniferous tubules within the testes. The tubules are separated by small clumps of interstitial tissue which contain the testosterone-secreting Leydig cells. This male hormone is responsible for many of the secondary sex characteristics of the male kangaroos. Its production is controlled via gonadotrophins produced in the pituitary gland at the base of the brain. Environmental factors may affect testicular function in kangaroos. Red kangaroos have impaired spermatogenesis in severe droughts.

The overall process of spermatogenesis has been studied in the tammar wallaby where the initial production in the testes takes 72–75 days. The sperm then passes into the epididymis where maturation and storage take place. During maturation changes occur which give the sperm the capacity for motility and the ability to recognise the ovum. This takes another 13 days. The epididymis is a much-coiled duct that lies within the scrotum and is enclosed with the testes by a membranous tunica vaginalis. The total length of the ductus epididymis in tammar wallabies is 35 metres. Three functional segments are recognised: the first concentrates the dilute spermatic fluid from the testes; the second is involved in maturation; and in the final segment storage occurs. Spermatozoa may remain viable in the final segment for about a month.

The semen of the ejaculate is derived from a series of accessory glands in addition to the contents of the epididymis. These accessory glands are the prostate and Cowper's glands (Fig. 5.5). The prostate in kangaroos is an obvious feature of the reproductive tract. It is a large, diffuse carrot-shaped gland that surrounds the urethra. It has three distinct segments which produce viscous fluids, presumably for aspects of maintenance of the spermatozoa. Three pairs of Cowper's glands occur in the kangaroos. They are bulbous structures covered in muscle and joined to the urethra by ducts. Their secretions are mucous in nature. Kangaroos are among the few marsupials that produce a true copulatory plug in the female tract: the semen coagulates shortly after its ejaculation. Whether the function of this plug is to block the passage of spermatozoa from subsequent matings with other males or to help in sperm transport in the female tract is unresolved.

## REPRODUCTIVE BEHAVIOUR

The reproductive behaviour of kangaroos in captivity has often been described. Under captive conditions species differences have been shown but they are not marked. For patterns of behaviour in the wild I have relied on observations made by David Croft at Fowlers Gap Research Station for details about red kangaroos and euros, and on those of Renata Jaremovic at

*Figure 5.6*
*Sexual checking of a female by an eastern grey male. Large males smell the pouch and cloaca of females that they meet and remain to follow those that are approaching oestrus.*

Bago State Forest in the southern highlands of New South Wales for details
about eastern grey kangaroos.

Red kangaroos show the least complex courtship activities. As with other
species, the most common sexual interaction is the sexual checking of the
females by males. The male approaches the female and sniffs her cloacal
region (Fig. 5.6) and occasionally her pouch opening. Young or mid-sized
males may be aggressively rejected but with dominant males she usually
just moves away if she is unreceptive — and that is usually the end of it.
David Croft noted that it was rare to see males touch or grasp such unin-
terested females. Red kangaroo females can be sparsely distributed and,
with no breeding season, are likely to come into oestrus at any time. To be
successful in breeding, the males must keep checking widely. Receptive
females often urinate when being checked and the males perform 'flehem'.
This occurs when a male sniffs the urine or puts his nose in it. He then
shakes his head and, with head lowered and stretched, strongly sniffs again.
This allows precise determination of the female's status. (Flehem is noticeably common in antilopine kangaroo males.) When coming into oestrus a
female also extends her area of activity so as to bring her condition to the
attention of more males. The aim is to attract the biggest male available.
Scent signals from such females presumably can be picked up at a considerable distance.

As oestrus nears, males show increased attention. Red kangaroo (and
euro) females at this time often have large young that are about to finally
leave the pouch. The male red kangaroo begins to follow, grasping and
stroking at the female's tail, usually high up near the butt. The full
sequence — 'male approaches, male sniffs, female moves off, male grasps
at the tail' — may be repeated several times, with the persistence of the
male increasing as she nears oestrus. A soft clucking sound is often made
by the male during this behaviour. Grey kangaroo (Plate 12) and euro males
follow this pattern and also often stand in front of the female, touching and
grasping her head, or give a high-standing display with an erect penis while
facing her. Antilopine kangaroo males may also move their body from side
to side when standing in front of or beside the female. 'Chesting', the male's
grasping of the female's head and rubbing it against his chest, is also done
by grey kangaroos but seemingly not by euros or red kangaroos.

When the female is about to ovulate the male stays close by, generally
within two or three metres. This consort relationship lasts for up to four
days. Often more than one male is in attendance — I have counted 14 but
more have been reported. The dominant male, usually the largest, eventually copulates with her. The female stands crouched with her back arched.
The male stands semi-erect behind the female, clasping her body with his
forearms tucked inside her thighs. He gives a short sequence of thrusts,
pulling the female back on to his penis. There may be frequent pauses

during the copulation, which generally lasts 10–15 minutes. Unlike other species, repeat copulations are rare among red kangaroos.

From this description it might seem that mating in red kangaroos is perfunctory. In fact, it can be anything but casual, due to the continued aggressive interference of the other attendant males and the attempts to drive them away.

Copulatory behaviour in euros is more complex than in red kangaroos. David Croft observed several matings in the wild (Plate 13). Extended bouts of copulation lasted over an hour. One time, six acts of copulation were observed, each lasting between a minute or so and 12 minutes. Two of the acts were terminated by interference from other males and once the copulating male was attacked and had to stop to fight off and chase the attacker. On the other occasions the female struggled and broke free. During the intervals between acts of copulation the male often grabbed and pulled at the female's head. He thrust his head to her and wiped his head on hers and along her body. Once the female lay down and the male attempted to pull her to her feet. The female was basically passive throughout and moved little except to break away from the male to terminate copulation. Her young at foot was nearby and twice attempted to approach but was cuffed by the male. After the final copulation the male remained to guard the female for several hours but the young was allowed to reapproach the female and suckle.

David Croft did see one consort euro male displaced. This occurred when 'Boss', the largest male in the area, arrived on the scene and displaced another large male. Boss was noted to be particularly aggressive, as well as large, and was invariably successful when it came to oestrus females (Plate 13).

The time over which large males maintain their status may differ between species of kangaroos. In eastern grey kangaroos a dominant male achieves tenure and maintains it, though it rarely lasts much more than a year. It is not uncommon for a male to die if seasonal conditions deteriorate, because maintenance of his status and constant reproductive activities require considerable energy. Feeding time is also much reduced and body condition falls. Much the same pattern is thought to occur in red kangaroos also, but the latter stages of the life of a dominant male red are little documented. Old grey-nosed males in poor condition persist at Fowlers Gap Station and, when tracked, seem to live in small areas. Their role in breeding, if any, is unclear. In areas where predation by dingos is significant these males may not last long.

The eastern grey's straightforward strategy may not be the most appropriate for euros. During his PhD work Tim Clancy tracked a large male (52 kg) for over two years. This euro seemed to take holidays from his duties as a dominant male. When he was in the hills he was clearly the successful consort male. However, on several occasions he left the hills and lived around Fowlers Gap Homestead in the creeklines and flats. When he returned to the hills, sometimes after several months, he resumed his position as the dominant male. Unfortunately, he was shot while raiding the Station vegetable garden so it was not possible to gauge how long he might have kept up this pattern.

The reason for this pattern of male euro breeding activity may be related to the fluctuating reproductive activity of female euros in the face of changing environmental conditions. At a large catch/release study at a waterhole on the edge of the hills during a dry summer we found that about 50 per cent of female euros were without pouch young and anoestrus as compared with only 14 per cent of red kangaroos. Vegetation conditions were not noticeably different throughout the area, nor were animal densities, and it appears that female euros withdraw from reproductive efforts in dry conditions sooner than do red kangaroos. It is during these conditions that the large males tend to leave both the hills and the euro females, who maintain their home-ranges in the rough country. Tim Clancy has suggested that the males may be extending their period of breeding success (but not the total number of copulations) in order to optimise their chances of producing young that survive to reproductive age. In a poor season most young that are conceived die, and many females are not breeding. The large dominant males, who have higher feeding requirements, choose to survive these conditions by moving to where the feed is better and leaving chancy breeding to the smaller males.

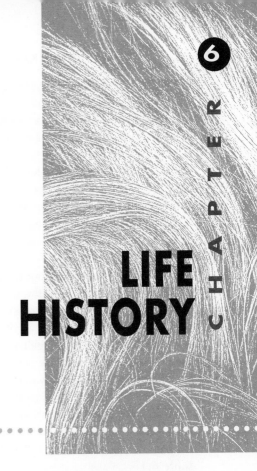

## CHAPTER 6

# LIFE HISTORY

## INTRODUCTION

Kangaroo species can either be continuous in their breeding or restrict their breeding to specific seasons. The timing of the early life of kangaroos is shown in Table 6.1. Where a species has a distinct breeding season the strategy is to ensure that the food supply is at its peak for the support of heavily lactating females and the weaning of young. With western grey kangaroos at Bakers Hill in the winter rainfall zone of Western Australia, more females raised young in years of good early autumn rains. In these years females easily sustain lactation and the young leave the pouch in late spring when feed is abundant and of high quality. With eastern grey kangaroos, the seasonal pattern is less pronounced in northern Australia but at Wallaby Creek in northern New South Wales Robyn Stuart-Dick still noted a peak period in the latter part of the year for the permanent emergence of young. The survival rate of these young is higher than that of those which emerge at other times of the year.

Antilopine kangaroos in tropical northern Australia have some births throughout the year, but in most cases breeding is timed so that young exit the pouch in the early part of the summer wet season, a time when nutritious grass is becoming readily available. Mating then occurs in the following months. David Croft noted little mating behaviour in the latter part of the wet season, February to March, and presumed that it had finished by then. Most young become independent by the end of the wet season, April to May. The black wallaroo is also found in this tropical area but there is limited information about its breeding patterns. Furred young have been reported in the pouch in the middle of the dry season, suggesting that pouch exit in this species also occurs at the beginning of the wet season. Aboriginal people still hunt black wallaroos and probably have unrecorded knowledge about the biology of this poorly understood kangaroo.

As in other aspects of their reproductive biology, grey kangaroos differ from the other species in timing their life cycle. Red kangaroos, wallaroos, the euro and antilopine kangaroos produce young substantially faster than do grey kangaroos. The course of development that enables young red kangaroos to finally leave the pouch after about 235 days takes some 320 days in grey kangaroos. The young of grey kangaroos, on leaving the pouch, are about the same size as the young of other species, so the growth rate of grey kangaroos is much slower. The reasons and implications are unclear. The different growth rates notwithstanding, overall patterns of pouch life and growth and development are similar in all species.

### Table 6.1
Breeding season and timing of the early life of kangaroos

| | Eastern grey | Western grey | Red | Eastern wallaroo | Euro | Antilopine |
|---|---|---|---|---|---|---|
| Birth season | Oct–Mar(a) | Oct–Mar | Contin. | Contin. | Contin. | Mar–April |
| Wt of young, g | 0.74 | 0.82 | 0.82 | – | 0.70 | 0.66 |
| 1st pouch exit, days | 283±24 | 298±34 | 185 | 213±8 | 201±10 | 210(b) |
| Permanent exit, days | 319±18 | 323±23(c) | 235±2 | 260±5 | 243±7 | 269±6 |
| Weaning, days | 540 | 540 | 360 | 351±58 | 409±74 | 380(b) |
| Sex maturity(d) | | | | | | |
|   females, mths | 18 | 14 | 15–20 | 20±3 | 21±3 | ? |
|   males, mths | 48 | 31 | 24 | 24 | 24 | ? |

(a) The pattern in northern New South Wales and Queensland is more variable.

(b) Values for antilopine kangaroos estimated by extrapolation from other aspects of their cycle.

(c) Subspecies differences occur.

(d) During poor seasonal conditions sexual maturity may be much delayed.

Values are means ± standard deviation.

# CARE OF THE YOUNG AND THEIR EARLY LIFE

The marsupial mode of reproduction focuses on lactation to nourish the poorly developed young. This means that the female kangaroo has extended responsibilities. Male kangaroos play no role in the raising of young. The single young is carried in a deep pouch until it reaches about 20 per cent of the mother's weight. Maternal behaviour may be divided into five stages: parturition; birth to the young's first emergence from the pouch; first emergence to permanent emergence; permanent emergence to weaning; the post-weaning period.

## PARTURITION

Parturition is not a trivial event even though the young is so small. As noted earlier, because it is so small and fragile it is important that the mother behave in such a way as to give the tiny young the best chance of reaching the pouch and attaching to a teat (Chapter 5). The behaviour of both mother and young is reflex; there is precise hormonal control of both the timing and the nature of the female's behaviour at the time of birth.

## EARLY POUCH LIFE

Much of our knowledge of the early life of kangaroos comes from Eleanor Russell who spent many patient hours watching the behaviour of joeys and their mothers. In the period between parturition and first emergence from the pouch the mother pays little attention to the tiny young (Plate 14) apart from pouch cleaning. The mother consumes the urine and faeces of the young and recycles about a third of the water used in milk production. Licking of its cloacal region stimulates urination and defaecation by the joey so the mother is able to directly clean up its excreta. As the young gets older it increases activity, wriggling and turning, so that a leg or the tail may protrude from the pouch. The mother seems rather unconcerned by this activity. Even when the joey starts to poke its head out of the pouch the mother's responses are relatively minor and restricted to some sniffing and grooming.

Most growth and development occurs in the latter half of pouch life. In the euro and wallaroos and in red kangaroos (Fig. 6.1) the young is continuously attached to the nipple until 120–130 days; during most of this time it is pink and naked, with eyes closed. Red kangaroo young start taking their first look at the outside world at 150 days, while it was 186 days before Robyn Stuart-Dick noted eastern grey joeys pushing their lightly furred heads out of the pouch.

At about 100 days the red kangaroo joey can be seen moving around in the pouch and this movement increases until near 150 days when the

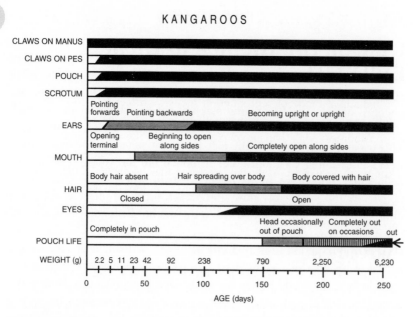

**Figure 6.1**
*Development of body characteristics and increase in weight of red kangaroos from birth to permanent pouch exit. Open bars indicate the absence of a character; black bars the presence of the character; intermediate stage shown as labelled or as a sloped line. After Sharman, Frith and Calaby (1964).*

young starts looking around the world. Its eyes have opened not long before this. The time from 'head first out' until the time the young starts getting out of the pouch at about 190 days is one of rapid growth. At this stage the young has only a light covering of hair. The limbs are growing fast and often project from the pouch as the young moves around. The mother now often licks the projecting parts and the young becomes more aware of her. It sniffs at her head, especially the muzzle, when she bends her head toward the pouch. The young spends an increasing amount of time with its head out of the pouch. It grooms itself, sniffs at its surroundings and later handles things on the ground. When the mother is grazing the young's head is brought close to the ground enabling it to try nibbling its first blades of grass (Plate 15).

## FIRST EMERGENCE FROM THE POUCH

From about 190 days the red kangaroo young, which now weighs about 2 kg, begins to leave the pouch. This is a much shorter time than in the grey kangaroos, which may take almost 100 days more (Robyn Stuart-Dick did, however, note eastern grey joeys out as early as 210 days during her Wallaby Creek studies). The young kangaroo first leaves the pouch in the typical way of macropodines: it falls out. However, the mother plays an active part in these events. She has control over the numerous muscles that control pouch size and opening. The entrance to the pouch has a semicircle of muscles on each side; when these are contracted the entrance is closed and the pouch is pulled up tight against the body, so the young is retained if the mother is alert or alarmed. Alternatively, the mother can really relax the pouch and its opening and let the joey fall out; she also can actively tip the young out by contracting the pouch.

Early excursions from the pouch are brief. They usually occur when mother is cleaning a relaxed pouch or is just lying relaxed. The young then may fall or 'ooze' out. In such circumstances the joey may only be partly out and not have to worry much about climbing back in if the relaxed pouch is agape. Also, the young may fall out by overbalancing: it simply stretches too far while exploring the world or trying to pick at some grass. This usually is the only way the joey leaves the pouch in the two or three weeks after initial vacation. Later in pouch life the young is sometimes deliberately tipped out by its mother, usually when she is cleaning the pouch. As the joeys grow they start to get out more often by their own efforts; they dive out head first when the mother is standing or just climb out if she is lying down.

The 'in-out' period from first emergence to permanent emergence is a period of life that placentals don't have. Kangaroos have the benefit of a good look at the world before having to face it permanently. During this period the mother still carries out pouch cleaning and grooming the joey — initially in, but later outside, the pouch. In addition, the mother's behaviour develops in relation to controlling the young when it leaves the pouch and also when it returns. She has general surveillance of the young and helps in its learning as it approaches permanent exit.

On the young's first exits from the pouch it stands (rather wobbly) where it falls, and then gets straight back into the pouch; the time out being less than a minute. In the first few weeks after initial pouch emergence the young may make frequent short excursions, which usually last no more than a couple of minutes and are rarely more than one or two metres from the mother. After these brave excursions the young returns to its mother and puts its head into the pouch. It may stand in this position and be groomed by the mother or it may get into the pouch by kicking off with its hind legs. The young does a complete somersault and ends up facing the pouch opening. For a big young this procedure is a major effort and there is much activity before comfort is reached; a bit of the tail or a leg often still protrudes.

For the young to get into the pouch the mother has to cooperate in a synchronised manner. Eleanor Russell videotaped the sequence for the tammar wallaby and the pattern is similar for kangaroos. As the young puts its head into the pouch and kicks off, the mother bends forward so that the pouch opening is brought closer to the ground. For small young the mother bends lower. The movement of the mother is crucial, since if she does not cooperate the young is left with its head and forelimbs in the pouch, kicking with its hind legs but unable to get over the lip of the pouch.

Return to the pouch is initiated by the young but sometimes the mother does not want to cooperate, notably if she is lying down resting. Then a bit of pestering is needed to get her to stand. The young sniffs at the pouch and scratches around the opening with its forepaws, trying to get its head in the pouch. It may even sniff and push at the mother's head. She may respond or not. The young also spends long periods at this age simply standing with its head in the pouch. This too requires cooperation. Apparently much of this behaviour is 'comfort' because suckling does not take place.

Late in the joey's pouch life the mother has a variety of ways of preventing or discouraging the young from entering the pouch. She may simply move away when the young puts its head inside. She may, more or less gently, push the young away or fail to cooperate by standing up if she was lying down. However, if something disturbs the mother she stands up quickly and calls and the young can be in the pouch in a couple of seconds.

In the final week before permanent exit the mother moves away from the young frequently but then stops and allows the young to catch up. The mother is training the young to readily recognise her and to follow when she moves off. By the time permanent pouch emergence occurs the young has also learnt that it will not be allowed back into the pouch unless there is some alarm. Finally the mother prevents the young from getting in and after a couple of days it stops trying.

## PERMANENT POUCH EMERGENCE

Growth is rapid in the 'in-out' phase of pouch life (Fig. 6.1, 6.2). At permanent pouch exit the young red kangaroo weighs some 4.5 kg, about 20 per cent of its mother's weight. Within 1–4 days of finally leaving the pouch for good the young of a red kangaroo or a member of the wallaroo group is generally replaced by a small new occupant. With the eastern grey kangaroo this replacement occurs after two weeks if a blastocyst was present.

The vacating young at foot still puts its head back into the pouch to suckle and continues to suckle on its usual teat for another four months (7–8 months or longer for grey kangaroos) but the level of suckling decreases as the young takes more herbage.

Once permanently out of the pouch a young at foot becomes more independent. It moves further away from the mother and for longer periods, but still follows her about and rests with her for much of the time. When alarmed, the young at foot relies on its mother to lead it from danger; it returns rapidly to her if anything untoward happens. The

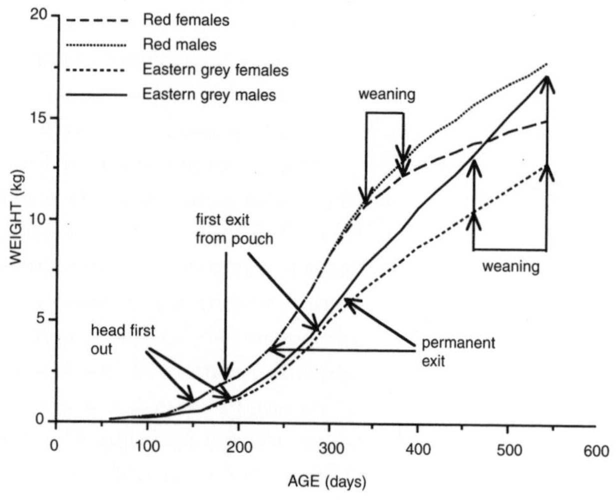

*Figure 6.2*
*Growth from birth to weaning in eastern grey kangaroos and red kangaroos under good conditions. There is much variability in the field and after pouch exit weight is a poor indicator of age. The grey kangaroos grow much more slowly at first, but with continued lactation they tend to catch up by the time they are weaned.*

mother does keep a watchful eye and calls and moves to her young if it becomes lost and gives its loud distress call. However, it seems that it is primarily the responsibility of the young to keep close to its mother. Mothers tend to have smaller home-ranges when they have small young at foot and are likely to stay away from their usual social groups. The young learn at this stage not to get too close to the other adults, especially males, who quickly chase them away.

## WEANING

The young at foot of red kangaroos and the wallaroo group are weaned at the end of their first year. The weaning time is often given as 365 days, but there is considerable variation. As weaning approaches, the young feeds from its mother less frequently. Eleanor Russell indicated that suckling occurred only two or three times in 24 hours. The young may pester the mother, but she increasingly ignores it and finally she prevents it from suckling at all. This period of weaning may take only a couple of days. In some cases, in all species, suckling is extended, especially with female young which may have a long association with their mothers. In these instances suckling may have a social rather than a nutritional purpose.

No marked change in the relationship between mother and young occurs at weaning. The separation is gradual and, at least in the case of female young, some recognition and association may continue well into adult life. At the beginning of this stage the young is still frequently associated with its mother, following her, lying with her and feeding and drinking with her. This pattern can persist until sexual maturity, with the mother and young still grooming and playfully sparring. At sexual maturity males tend to leave their mothers, but whether they all disperse widely is not clear. Female kangaroos also seem to wander at this stage, but many eventually set up home-ranges near their mother and so may still be part of her group or mob. With grey kangaroos this association is obvious. Daughters may never disperse far and may well continue to be part of the basic 'group'. Sons usually disperse from their mother's home-range one to two years after weaning.

Differences in the care of female and male young have been suggested. The female kangaroo seems to play an active role in the rearing process and to make different energy investments depending on the sex of the offspring and the environmental conditions. This suggestion of differential investment is related to the notion that, while a daughter will probably produce a few young in her life, a successful male can produce many. At Wallaby Creek Robyn Stuart-Dick showed that pre-weaning investment (time given to weaning) by female eastern grey kangaroos is not generally different for males and females, but if males were weaned early they had a poorer chance of survival. Of note, post-weaning investment was greater for female young, with mothers being more active in maintaining their association with their daughters. This was offset by a greater production of sons in good seasons. Males can take advantage of good seasons since a male's expected lifetime reproductive success is likely to be influenced by rapid early growth and good physical condition. How the mother influences the sex ratios of pouch young is unclear.

Recently at Fowlers Gap Research Station Debbie Ashworth, a PhD student working with David Croft, found another pattern of differential investment, in euros. Euro females are conservative in their reproductive activities and stop breeding earlier during drought than do red kangaroos. Even so, following poor rainfall in 1991 only about half the pouch young survived to weaning. The majority of deaths were in the eighth month — just prior to, or at, pouch exit. This is the time of maximum growth and highest lactational demand on the mothers. In these conditions mothers put more effort (energy) into the raising of a male, perhaps in the 'hope' of producing a large successful male. This differential investment was indicated by the observation that mothers which successfully rear a male young are much less likely to successfully rear the next young because of declining body condition. If the previous young was a male only 50 per cent or so of the next young were successfully reared, as compared with 86 per cent if the previous surviving offspring was a female. The mothers did appear to compensate the female young by letting them associate longer. Males associate with the mothers for six or seven months after pouch emergence, compared with about nine months for females; daughters have been seen in the company of their mothers for over 3.5 years.

It has been suggested that females may even terminate the life of a pouch young if it is the 'wrong' sex for the times. Such behaviour has often been suggested as a good reproductive strategy, but it has been difficult to demonstrate. Debbie Ashworth found that in poor times euro mothers reared fewer males. While the sex ratio at birth is 1:1, in drought females formed a higher proportion of the pouch inhabitants. The suggestion is that mothers dispose of some male young at a very early age, perhaps within the first couple of weeks.

## LACTATION

Lactation in kangaroos provides all the nutrients and energy for growth and development during most of pouch life, this being about eight months duration for red kangaroos, wallaroos and euros and some ten months for the grey kangaroos. Joeys are not weaned until four months (for red kangaroos and wallaroos/euros) to eight months (for grey kangaroos) after leaving the pouch. The benefits derived from lactation can be seen by the growth rates of pouch young (Fig. 6.2). The newborn of kangaroos are less than a gram in weight, but by the time of permanent emergence from the pouch

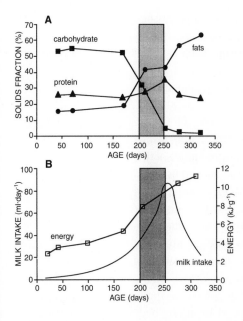

**Figure 6.3**
*Changes in (A) the composition and (B) the energy content and volume of milk produced by a mother tammar wallaby, Macropus eugenii, from birth of a young to its weaning. Kangaroos are likely to show a similar pattern. The period between first emergence from pouch and permanent exit is shown by the shaded bar. Peak milk production, with elevated fats (for energy) and proteins (for growth), occurs at permanent pouch exit; thereafter herbage intake increases rapidly. Derived from Merchant (1989).*

they are 4–5 kg. As noted earlier, the growth rate of the eastern grey kangaroo is much slower than that of the red kangaroo but, because of the longer time the grey spends in the pouch, the exit weights are similar (Fig. 6.2). In the period from exit until weaning the young's body more than doubles in weight. Again, the relatively slower growth rate of the eastern grey kangaroo is compensated for by the later weaning of the young.

Rate of growth is to some degree controlled by the milk supply, since rate of growth of pouch young is reduced in drought. The reverse is also seen if small pouch young are fostered into the pouch of a female that is in a more advanced stage of lactation; then growth rate is enhanced. Detailed information on milk production is not available for kangaroos but the available data suggest that it follows the pattern known for the smaller tammar wallaby (4–5 kg) (Fig. 6.3). In the tammar wallaby, 30 days after birth, milk production was only 1 ml/day. This increased to 9 ml/day at day 130, to 43 ml/day at day 210 and to a peak of 86 ml/day at day 250 — at the end of pouch life when the growth rate of the joey was at its highest. Not only was the quantity of milk produced markedly increased but many of its characteristics were also changed. The energy content increased from 2.5 kJ/ml at day 7 to a peak of 11.2 kJ/ml at day 250. An increase in fat content accounts for much of the increase in energy content. The reduction in volume of the milk towards final weaning is compensated for by the young's increasing herbage consumption.

Composition of the milk is tailored to the requirements of the developing young. An example is the increase in sulphur-containing amino acids around the time of hair formation; hair has a high content of sulphur-containing proteins. Since milk is the only source of nutrients and micronutrients, e.g. vitamins, it is presumed that their levels in the milk are adjusted to meet the differing requirements of the young as it grows. The mechanism for these adjustments is unknown. One specific function of the milk appears to be the transfer of immunity to the newborn. At birth the young has little immunity, yet the pouch is not sterile. Around birth the mammary glands secrete a clear fluid that has free-floating cells and maternal immunoglobulins; this is similar to the colostrum of placentals. Thus immunological protection is provided in this early milk.

The changing characteristics of the milk with the progression of pouch life brings us to another remarkable feature of kangaroo physiology: the simultaneous production of two milks of completely different characteristics at one time. This occurs when a birth takes place before the young at foot has been weaned. The obvious example of this is in the continuous breeding of red kangaroos, wallaroos and euros. It is also seen in the seasonal breeding of the two grey kangaroos, due to their relatively delayed weaning of the young at foot. In such conditions milk has to be provided for a newborn weighing about one gram and for a young at foot weighing more than 4 kg.

If the pattern of milk volume and composition (Fig 6.3) is considered, the functional problem is readily appreciated. For one thing, it is obvious that the two active teats are required to act independently. How this uniquely macropodoid feature occurs is not well understood. It has been suggested that the milk let-down hormone, oxytocin, is involved via different sucking stimuli. The small, permanently attached young presumably exerts only a slight sucking pressure compared to its much larger sibling, the young at foot. Yet the overall process of lactation is very complex and so it would be expected that its fine control would also be complex.

## FROM WEANING TO SEXUAL MATURITY

### RED KANGAROOS

Most males are able to produce sperm at about 3 years old, at 20–25 kg. However, the age of sexual maturity can vary with seasonal conditions and regions. In studies of captive animals under optimal conditions, some males were producing sperm at 2 years of age. On the other hand, in arid regions maturity may be delayed until 4 years according to Harry Frith and Geoff Sharman (Fig. 6.4). As noted before, kangaroos, especially males, grow throughout most of their lives. The males grow most rapidly around the onset of sexual maturity (Fig. 4.2) and reach 40 kg near 5 years of age. In some districts where numbers are low due to drought or predation males at 5 years of age may be successful in breeding, yet in other areas they may have to survive another 5–7 years and grow to 70 kg before they are able to make a significant contribution to breeding. This is the case at Fowlers Gap Station.

As with males, the age at which females reach sexual maturity varies with environmental conditions, mainly the availability of suitable good feed. Young female red kangaroos in captivity reach sexual maturity at 15–20 months. In the extensive field study conducted

**Figure 6.4**
*Influence of seasonal conditions on the ages at which red kangaroo females reach sexual maturity in the wild. Male development is also affected, but sample size was not sufficient to provide a clear pattern. After Frith and Sharman (1964).*

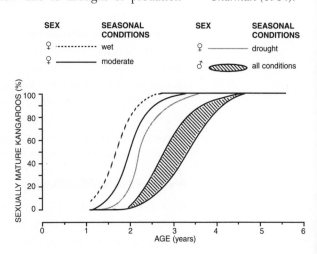

by Frith and Sharman it was found that under good conditions some females were mature at 17 months old (Fig. 6.4), but that some 4-year-old animals were not yet mature. In another study made during drought at Cunnamulla, Queensland, no females were sexually mature before 20–24 months old and many females 4.5–5 years of age were not sexually mature.

## WALLAROOS AND THE EURO

Bill Poole and Jim Merchant conducted long-term studies of yard colonies and demonstrated little difference in the onset of sexual maturity of the two common subspecies of *Macropus robustus* — the eastern wallaroo and the euro. More field information is available for the euros.

The age at which euro males achieve active spermatogenesis is about 2 years when they weigh about 15 kg. As with the red and grey kangaroos, a significant role in the breeding population does not come for some years, until they reach 40 kg at more than 7 years of age. The results obtained by Tim Ealey from the north of Western Australia indicate that euro males undergo a spurt in weight and become more muscular at about 5–6 years, a time when limb bone lengths are reaching maximum size. This has the appearance of the 'filling out' seen in human males when they reach their late teens. It is not long after this that euros begin to achieve some success in mating, if the 'boss' is away. Tim Clancy observed instances at Fowlers Gap Station where single smaller males, weighing less than 35 kg, were consorts to oestrus females and successfully copulated with them. However, if a larger male came on the scene they were displaced. The rough hilly nature of the habitat of the euro may enable the younger males to have more breeding success than occurs in other species.

The reproductive development of female euros is variable. Ealey noted that in the Pilbara district of Western Australia euros were not known to breed under 2 years old and during poor seasons breeding was deferred further. In such circumstances there were 4-year-old females that had not bred. In optimal circumstances (CSIRO captive colonies) females have bred at just over 14 months old, but even under these conditions some are not mature until 2 years old. The basic pattern of sexual maturity is shown in Table 6.1. The first sign of sexual maturity is the eversion of the teats. Irrespective of the female's age its pouch retains its juvenile characteristics, remaining small, tight and dry, until the teats begin to evert.

## ANTILOPINE KANGAROOS

Little is known of the onset of sexual maturity in antilopine kangaroos. In some aspects they resemble the wallaroos and euros and consequently, where data are lacking, the growth and development patterns seen in these related species are taken as a guide. Animals estimated to be as old as 16 years have been reported in field shot samples so no doubt they live to an age of about 20 years.

## GREY KANGAROOS

*Males — early growth and development*
The basic development patterns in the two grey kangaroos is similar, but there are some differences. The patterns revealed in yard studies probably reflect optimum conditions and they give a base-line. For males reproductive maturity first occurs after about 2.5 years in western grey kangaroos; but it occurs later, about 4 years, in eastern greys. Western grey kangaroos weigh about 25 kg at this stage and it is at this time that their association with their mother breaks down. Some may disperse now, but they do not necessarily breed yet. Generally males are not considered adult until they are 45–50 kg and start to get the obvious male body conformation. For western grey kangaroos this occurs at 5 years old; in a normal field situation they would not be expected to make a significant contribution to breeding until they were 55–60 kg or 6–7 years old. The survivorship curves for male western greys (Fig. 6.5) indicate that very few males, about 5 per cent, reach this phase of life in the wild. Males older than 10 years are rare in the wild.

The reason for the high mortality of male eastern and western grey kangaroos is not well understood. While about half of the females die before they reach breeding age, many more males die before they are full adults. The initial die-off occurs between permanent pouch exit and weaning. It continues until the young are about 3 years. The pattern of mortality for western grey kangaroos at Bakers Hill in Western Australia is such that, while 83 per cent of mature females had pouch young, only 27 per cent also had a young at foot.

Similar patterns have been observed for other kangaroo species and this may be the main regulator of population size. While predation by dingos (where they overlap in range), foxes and eagles may have an impact, food is probably the limiting factor. It is simply a lack of available energy that is behind the high mortality. The population trends at Kinchega National Park (NSW) (Fig. 6.6) show that in good years many young survive but in drought years recruitment to the population is very small. The young need much good feed to grow rapidly; their digestive systems are not able to cope with the poorer quality feed that adults can handle. The reason for the male-biased mortality is unclear but it may be that in poor times the mother may choose

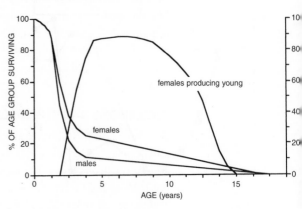

**Figure 6.5**
*Survivorship of male and female western grey kangaroos at Bakers Hill in the wandoo woodland of Western Australia. Also shown is the change in fertility of females with age. The number of females in an age class that produce young declines markedly beyond 8 years of age. After Arnold et al. (1991).*

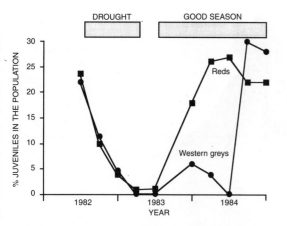

DROUGHT    GOOD SEASON

Reds

Western greys

1982    1983    1984
YEAR

% JUVENILES IN THE POPULATION

**Figure 6.6**
*Percentage of juveniles in the populations of red kangaroos and western grey kangaroos through a drought and the following good season at Kinchega National Park. The decrease of juveniles of both species during the drought was largely due to juvenile mortality and eventually a cessation of breeding. The delayed increase in numbers of juvenile western greys was due to the drought breaking **after** their spring–summer breeding season. Red kangaroos are continuous breeders if seasonal conditions allow. Derived from Shepherd (1987).*

to invest less energy in her male offspring than in female joeys. Alternatively, males may simply require more feed to grow bigger. They may put their nutritional intake initially into bone and muscle with little going into fat, thereby putting themselves at risk if environmental conditions deteriorate. This problem would be compounded by males also being more active.

*Females — growth and development* In female western grey kangaroos the onset of sexual maturity in captive populations came at 14–18 months. As sexual maturity is approached the teats gradually evert and the pouch increases in size. The time between full eversion of the teats and the first oestrus is not consistent, but the two events occur within a few weeks. At this stage the pouch becomes covered with a brown waxy secretion. This secretion, when it builds up, is removed by bouts of pouch cleaning, usually by licking. Such cleaning is most active before oestrus or birth. The area around the teats is cleaned first and then the rest of the pouch.

For western grey kangaroos, breeding in the field rarely occurs before 2 years of age when body weight is about 16 kg. At Bakers Hill the full population was breeding at a weight of 24 kg, about 3 years old. Once breeding, most females had young annually. The fertility of females declined after 7–8 years and by 12 years of age few females bred (Fig. 6.5).

Eastern grey kangaroo females in the wild also start to breed at a much later age than in yard studies. Several yard studies indicate that first breeding may start at about 2 years old but, in detailed field observations at Wallaby Creek in northern New South Wales, Robyn Stuart-Dick found that first conception did not occur until 3–3.5 years. Density of animals and also seasonal conditions have marked influences. As in western greys, age of breeding tends to be younger in the semi-arid regions during good seasons, as compared with stable populations in higher rainfall districts. Also, under good conditions the proportion of young which survive is greater in semi-arid regions.

## SOCIAL ASPECTS OF THE LIFE OF KANGAROOS

Social structure can be identified from social interactions. There are three broad categories of social interaction: non-aggressive (non-agonistic in scientific terms), aggressive/submissive (agonistic) and sexual. The latter category was discussed in Chapter 5.

**Figure 6.7**
*Nose sniffing is a common non-agonistic social behaviour. It often occurs when an animal joins a group. Kangaroos obviously gain much information from smell cues.*

## Non-agonistic behaviour

Non-agonistic interactions are social actions that do not involve aggression or obvious reproductive behaviour. Such interactions are likely to promote the 'togetherness' of a group of kangaroos — but agonistic or sexual behaviour may well follow.

Non-agonistic behaviour includes mutual nose touching and sniffing; licking the lips of another; other touching and sniffing (non-sexual); grooming other individuals; social play; and nuzzling the pouch of a female. Mutual nose touching and sniffing (Fig. 6.7) is carried out with the heads extended and is often seen when a kangaroo joins a group. Sniffing brings animals close together, generally without consequent aggression. Sometimes during mutual sniffing one animal will hold its body closer to the ground and its head will quiver. This animal is often the smaller of the two interacting and the action may indicate submission. Kangaroos obviously gain much information about other individuals from smell cues. Non-agonistic behaviour establishes a network of relationships between age groups and the two sexes. Non-agonistic actions from male to female are particularly common, with males usually approaching females. Larger males are most involved in meeting females.

Other non-agonistic social behaviour occurs largely between mother and young. Grooming is a case in point; usually with the mother grooming a young at foot, often while it is suckling or just after suckling. With red

**Figure 6.8**
*Agonistic social interactions: (A) the high-standing threat display of a large male kangaroo; (B) play fighting between a mother and her young (this is a complex behaviour with both agonistic and non-agonistic implications).*

kangaroos and euros mutual grooming is confined to mother and young. Such grooming reinforces the mother–young bond, as it does in primates. Nuzzling of the pouch by the young is another such interaction but in this case it is the young that initiates the behaviour. It is often associated with the young trying to gain access to the pouch or just to the nipple in order to suckle. At times, however, the young may simply put its head into the pouch for a few seconds, perhaps seeking reassurance. The mother will push the young away if she is not to be bothered. Licking the lips is another action of the young at foot. The young may lick the lips of the mother for several minutes, apparently collecting saliva. This behaviour may result in the passage of digestive micro-organisms to the soon-to-be-weaned young, which will have to come to rely on fermentative digestion of vegetation for its nutrition.

Social play is also usually confined to mother–young interactions. (However, among the more gregarious species such as eastern grey kangaroos and, especially, antilopine kangaroos, young subadults interact and play together.) Most social play takes the form of play-fighting (Fig. 6.8). Mother and young grasp each other around the neck and grapple. There is touching of forepaws, with some kicking by the young. The interaction may be started by either mother or young. The mother is 'training' the young for life as an adult — young males which engage in this behaviour are more involved in play-fighting. Young at foot commonly play by themselves. They hop rapidly around their mother or away from her and back again. It seems as if they are testing their legs, without getting too far away from mother. They also pick up twigs and bits of grass and play with them; grappling with bushes is another play activity.

## AGONISTIC SOCIAL INTERACTIONS

Agonistic (aggressive) or asocial interactions bring to mind the spectacular fights of large males, but in reality such dramatic interactions are rare in the wild. Most agonistic encounters are one-sided and finish quickly. A kangaroo at which aggression is directed usually moves away without challenge. Submissive displays are often hard to identify in the field because they are subtle and may be indicated merely by slight changes in posture or in head and ear position. The submissive 'cough' given by eastern grey kangaroos or the clucking sounds of wallaroos and euros are not heard from red kangaroos, although immature and female red kangaroos do make a rapid staccato clicking sound if attacked by larger animals; this sound is similar to the distress vocalisation of small young at foot. A threatened animal does not always retreat, especially if it is of similar size, and a fight may ensue.

Two main types of agonistic interaction, supplanting encounters and fighting, were observed by David Croft in his studies of red kangaroos and euros at Fowlers Gap Station.

*Supplanting encounters* Supplanting encounters were more common than fights and could be active or passive. In passive situations an approached animal just gets out of the way quickly. In active displacement an obvious aggressive act is involved. Such acts are threatening postures, pushes, hits and chases. Supplanting behaviour occurs for a variety of reasons. The most common reason is to gain access to a 'lying up' place and to maintain 'personal space' by removing another animal which is too close. This motive obtains among euros where there is competition for favoured shady caves and rock overhangs at times of summer heat. Croft noted a high level of aggression around good caves at Fowlers Gap Station. Euros do not share small caves unless they are unable to displace the initial occupant; the tolerance distance between animals is about one metre. I have seen eight euros of mixed sexes and sizes come out of one small cave, but this was at a time of very hot dry conditions. Success in disputes about lying-up sites is generally related to the animal's size. Full-blown fights can erupt between well-matched kangaroos. Croft observed a fight over the use of a cave in which a male euro pushed another off a 3 m high ledge. Access to food or water and of course access to oestrus females are other factors which are involved in aggressive interactions between kangaroos.

*Threat displays* A threat is usually indicated by posture and it serves to indicate an intention to act aggressively. Three patterns of threat behaviour are generally shown, among all species of kangaroo: upright postures, stiff-legged walking, and object manipulation (mainly grass or bush pulling).

An upright stance is the most common threat observed in the wild. The kangaroo stands up straight (Fig. 6.8) with its forearms outstretched. This is usually sufficient to displace a smaller animal, but if the kangaroo to which the attention is directed does not respond or is of a similar size a high-standing posture is adopted. The kangaroo then stretches itself up to its fullest height, standing on tiptoe and balancing on the tip of the tail; the forearms are extended, ready to strike.

Another dramatic posture is high standing with the head thrown well back; one foreleg is stretched out and the other is touching or scratching the chest. This behaviour is more common in males but females do show it, often with both forepaws scratching the chest. David Croft was hesitant to call this a threat display because it occurred in a variety of other contexts. He suggested that it might have the message 'Here I am, look how big I am!'.

Stiff-legged walking is seen in males. The aggressor stands with his body supported on the tip of the tail, hind toes and forepaws; the legs are spread wide and the back is highly arched. The threatening animal commonly circles his opponent. The display is usually seen in adult males of similar size when the opponent will neither fight nor retreat. But fighting often eventuates. At times no specific reason for such activity is immediately obvious and it is possible that dominance is being established.

Object manipulation such as grass pulling is a conspicuous threat display among males. Bushes are also pulled and grappled with in patterns similar to fighting, or a male may thrust his chest into a bush or grass clump and move his neck back and forth rubbing it and the chest. Apart from being used in threat displays grass pulling can be seen in groups of males, including smaller individuals among whom fights do not develop, and in the course of sexual encounters when other males are not present; the intent at these times is a matter of debate.

In supplanting encounters the common method of active displacement is a push. The animal to be moved is grasped, often around the middle, and pushed away. Pushing is often accompanied by an aggressive 'ha' vocalisation. In more vigorous situations the aggressor hits the other animal with its forepaw and may even chase and continue to hit the fleeing animal.

Usually an aggressor uses the upright threat stance before hitting — but not when a mother hits a young. The 'ha' sound may be used also as a warning when another animal is approaching a resource that is being utilised, e.g shade or feed.

## FIGHTING

Fighting has been described in many species of kangaroos and wallabies, especially the ritualised fighting of males popularly referred to as 'boxing' (Fig. 6.9). Fighting can be either brief or prolonged and ritualised. Out in the wild, brief fights are relatively rare except in highly competitive situations — such as between consort males and their competitors for access to an oestrus female, or at limited drinking sites in hot weather. Both sexes may be involved in the latter case. The form of these short sharp clashes is similar to that of the longer ritualised fights of males, except that locking of the forearms is rare.

The ritualised fighting or 'boxing' of kangaroos is primarily a male behaviour. Abbreviated bouts also occur between mothers and their young in social play (Fig. 6.8), so that the motor patterns are established at an early age. Initiation of boxing contests can sometimes occur with a minimum of fuss. Males may be standing or grazing near each other when suddenly they rear up and start grappling and fighting. More commonly, fights are

*Figure 6.9*
*Fighting in male eastern grey kangaroos. Fighting is a ritualised behaviour with much wrestling and kicking in a high-standing position.*

preceded by the opponents scratching and grooming their sides and chests a good deal, and often one or both contestants will adopt the high-standing posture. The point at which a fight begins is usually when one animal grasps the neck of the other with its forepaws (Fig. 6.9). Even at this stage a challenge is not always accepted. Large males often reject the challenge from smaller males, acting as if they do not care to be bothered by an inferior opponent.

Fights generally follow a predictable direction. The combatants usually adopt the high-standing posture (though a large male may stand flat-footed if fighting a small animal) and paw at each other's head, shoulders and chest. The claws of the forepaws are extended. During this pawing heads are thrown back, which protects the eyes and ears from the raking claws. At this stage the combatants are locked together by their forearms. From this locked forearm position males push and wrestle with each other. Frequently one animal balances on its tail and kicks its opponent's abdomen with its strong hind legs. This can be very vigorous; I have been able to hear the sound of such kicks from about 150 metres away. Often there are frequent pauses in a fight, during which the kangaroos maintain their high-standing/forearms locked position. Vocalisation by fighting red kangaroos seems to be rare but eastern grey kangaroos do vocalise during fights. Breaks in fights occur, and then the males vigorously groom and scratch themselves.

Who are the winners in such contests? Basically, a clear winner is decided when one animal breaks off the fight and retreats. The winners usually have more strength. They are able to push their opponents backwards or down to the ground. They are seen also to grasp their opponents when they break contact and push them away. The initiators of fights are generally the winners.

Of note, it is the losers that kick more frequently. From his detailed observations at Fowlers Gap Station David Croft suggests that losers kick in order to parry the vigorous thrusts of the eventual winner. If the potential destructive capacity of the kick were utilised aggressively rather than defensively it would be expected that winners, not losers, would kick more frequently. Deaths have occurred from kicking in captive colonies and this may be because the loser cannot retreat.

Why do these ritualied fights occur? In the wild Croft noted that there was usually no obvious benefit from winning a contest. I have seen several fights take place in the vicinity of an oestrus female; however, it was among the smaller males that these fights occurred; the large male in consort with the female was not involved. It is probable that such ritualised fights are instrumental in the establishment of dominance patterns. It has been observed that the winner of a fight may, later in the day, displace the loser from a lying-up site.

## DOMINANCE PATTERNS

Dominance hierarchies are established readily in captive colonies where animals are forced into close association; and much of the study of social interaction has been carried out in these situations. Eleanor Russell has shown that in such conditions size and age determine an animal's rank. Even in these artificial conditions red kangaroos are relatively tolerant animals and the level of agonistic interaction is low. The highest ranking animals lead relatively peaceful lives since they are not subject to aggression and are not very aggressive themselves. David Croft confirmed this pattern in field studies, again noting the very tolerant nature of this species. From his work it was seen that males ranked largely according to size. Size was also significant in relation to intersex ranking, with large and medium males being dominant over females. Among females of similar size and age reproductive condition may be significant in determining status. Young at foot never act aggressively toward adults or subadults except in play situations. Medium-sized males are mostly involved in non-aggressive behaviour with each other. Croft suggests that this is an early part of the process whereby these animals get to know each other and determine their places in the dominance pattern. Fighting is the extreme element of this process designed eventually to gain dominant access to females.

# LIVING IN THE ENVIRONMENT — FEEDING

Although modern kangaroos eat a variety of plants they are predominantly grass eaters. This may not seem unusual but the evolution of the anatomical and physiological specialisation that allow this feeding pattern has been a complex process. Only ruminants, like cattle and antelopes, and a few species of leaf-eating monkeys have similar adaptations to those found in kangaroos.

## OF TEETH AND CHEWING

The ancestral marsupials were mouse-sized insectivorous animals. Their teeth, like those of modern small dasyurid marsupials, were designed to break through the tough exoskeleton of insects and to cut them up into small pieces for rapid digestion (Fig. 7.1). While some plant material can be part of the diet of such animals, they are not equipped to eat grass, which is much more fibrous than most other leafy plants. The rat-kangaroos give some indication of the evolutionary progression toward specialised grazing (Fig. 7.1). These small members of the kangaroo family eat animals, such as invertebrates and small lizards, and a variety of vegetable matter; their cutting premolar and crushing molar teeth reflect this. The plants or plant parts that they eat are not, however, the mature grasses that may be included in the diet of large kangaroos.

Teeth have two functions, biting and chewing. The teeth of kangaroos are highly specialised in both respects. The front incisors are involved in the initial selection and biting off of food. The two rows of molars chop and grind the food (Fig. 7.1).

The incisors determine the size and shape of the 'bite' and thus the food available to an animal. A narrow 'delicate' set of incisors enable a grazing mammal to take short and sparse pasture. Larger animals with bigger 'bites' are favoured by taller and denser pasture, even if it is of poor quality. This is seen in the different feeding patterns of sheep and cattle, with which pastoralists are familiar. Kangaroos are the marsupial equivalent of sheep (and also deer) in this respect, since their 'bite' is small.

When a kangaroo takes a bite the lower jaw slides forward as the mouth opens and the feed is seized in the overlapping incisors. The food is then detached by a jerk of the animal's head; it is not just cut off. An unusual aspect of the bite of kangaroos is that the two sides of the lower jaw are not fixed together and the two protruding large lower incisors separate during the bite (Fig. 7.2). This separation increases the lower incisor surface that can be opposed to the upper incisors, and the harder the bite the wider the separation. It was once thought that these movable lower incisors provided a scissor action to cut grass, but this is a 'marsupial myth'.

Once taken in, the food is organised by the tongue and lips and passed back to the molar teeth. The molar teeth of the kangaroos chop up (shear) the fibrous grass into small particles so that a large surface area is provided throughout the material in order to speed digestion. The molar tooth row of kangaroos is arched and chewing is usually limited to about the second and third teeth in the row. The limited area used means that more force can be brought to bear in the shearing action. Kangaroos alternate the side of the mouth on which they chew. This also concentrates the shearing action, which is further enhanced by special lengthwise ridges (links) on the molars. The molars of kangaroos differ from those of most wallabies, which lack these lengthwise links (Fig. 7.2). Wallabies primarily eat leafy, softer vegetation, which is less fibrous than grass. Their molar teeth crush the vegetation rather than finely chopping it.

The cutting surfaces of molar teeth wear down and need to be maintained. As well as the dust and grit on any vegetation grass contains

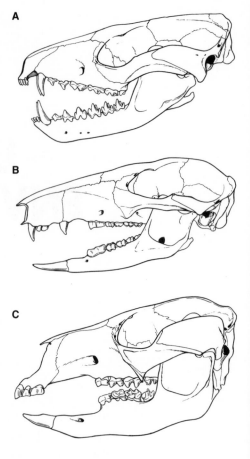

**A**

**B**

**C**

**Figure 7.1**
*Marsupial skulls showing specialisations of the teeth for different diets: (A) spotted-tailed quoll, an insectivorous/carnivorous dasyurid with cutting teeth; (B) long-nosed potoroo, an omnivorous rat-kangaroo with cutting and crushing teeth; (C) euro, a grazing kangaroo with teeth specialised for chopping and grinding grass.*

*Figure 7.2*
*Functional aspects of kangaroo teeth: (A) the arrangement in euros of the upper and lower incisors during the bite — the lower incisors separate (right) during a hard bite; (B) molar teeth of a browsing swamp wallaby; (C) molar teeth of an eastern grey kangaroo showing grass-cutting links between the lophs. Both types of molars are shown in occlusion on the right. Drawn from original specimens. See Sanson (1989) for discussion and references.*

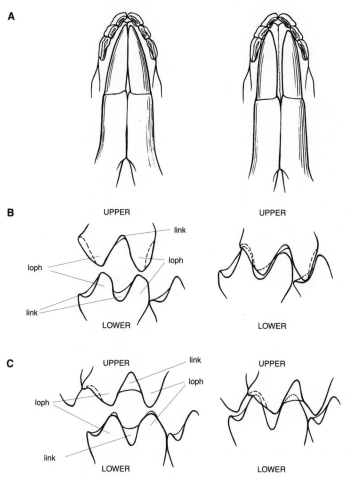

mineral silica. This appears to be part of its 'defence' against herbivores. In placental herbivores tooth wear is counteracted by continuous growth of the molars. Kangaroos cope differently with the problem, having a unique pattern of movement of the molars in the jaw. As teeth are worn they move forward and are shed from the jaw (Fig. 7.3). This 'molar progression' means that eventually all but the rear molars are lost. The age of kangaroos can be determined from the extent of molar progression. After a series of good seasons I once saw an old doe with only two very worn molars on each of her jaws.

Equations to determine the approximate age of some kangaroo species were derived in 1965 by Tom Kirkpatrick, then with the Queensland Department of Primary Industries. The equations are from meaurements made on the palate of cleaned skulls and relate to the progression of the molars relative to the front rim of the orbit of the eye. The molar index (M.I.)

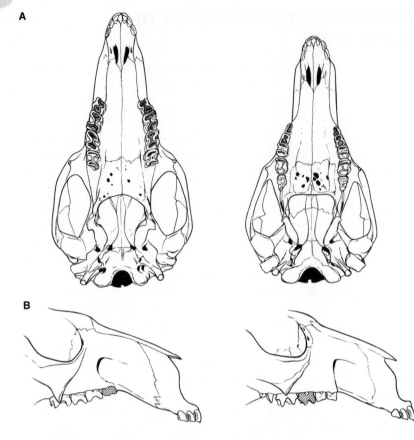

**A**

**B**

**Figure 7.3**

**Figure 7.3**
*(A) The skulls of an old euro (left) and a young red kangaroo, showing the upper teeth. The euro with four worn molars is 16–17 years old, the 4th molar having moved forward so that it is completely past the front rim of the eye orbit. In the younger red kangaroo (aged 3 years) two deciduous premolars are present and the 3rd molar is still erupting. The 3rd molar is about one-third past the front of the orbit. (B) The skulls seen from the side. The downward-pointing zygomatic process has also been used as a reference point in aging by molar progression. The first molar is shaded. (See text for Kirkpatrick's (1965) aging equations.)*

is an estimate of how many molars and parts of molars have progressed past this point. An M.I. of 2.5 would mean that the 1st and 2nd molars and half the 3rd molar were forward of the front rim of the orbit. The equations have 95 per cent confidence limits of about ±15–20 per cent of estimated age and are:

Eastern grey — log age (days) = 2.4546±0.2934 M.I.

Eastern wallaroo — log age (days) = 2.2972±0.3488 M.I.

Red kangaroo — log age (days) = 2.211±0.3604 M.I.

Kangaroos do not chew their cud, as do sheep and cattle, to increase the breakup of feed. Those ruminants do not initially chew their food as finely as kangaroos do, but rechew it later 'at their leisure'. A form of regurgitation does occur irregularly in kangaroos that are fed fibrous feed or fresh grass. It involves strong 'hiccups' and some food may be regurgitated into the mouth, but this is quickly reswallowed, not rechewed. The term 'merycism' has been suggested to describe this process. It appears to be of little importance in digestion.

# MICROBIAL FERMENTATION OF PLANT FIBRE

Tough carbohydrate polymers, such as cellulose, maintain the structure of plants. These polymers give strength to cell walls and support vessels, and may make up a large proportion of some plants. Mammals do not have the right enzymes to digest these complex carbohydrates, which are generally referred to as plant fibre. However, kangaroos, sheep and cattle, which graze open grasslands, are largely dependent for their energy on this part of the vegetation. So how is digestion accomplished in these species?

Most animals that feed on plants accomplish fibre digestion by an association with micro-organisms. Specialised bacteria are most common but protozoa and fungi can also participate. This process is called 'symbiosis' and it is a relationship that provides both organisms with a benefit. Kangaroos (and ruminants) have a large expanded chamber in the forepart of their gut where such symbiotic digestion occurs. The process is fermentation, which is the breakdown of food in the absence of oxygen; in other words anaerobic metabolism. Without oxygen food cannot be fully broken down ('burnt') and all energy made available. The micro-organisms get energy and nutrients to carry out their life activities but with virtually no oxygen in the forestomach they can utilise only a small amount of the energy from the fibre. Their excretory products still contain much of that energy, and it is these that are absorbed and metabolised by the kangaroos. These compounds are the short-chain fatty acids such as acetic, butyric and proprionic acids. The kangaroo gets only some 70 per cent of the energy out of the digested plant fibre but this is better than nothing.

If microbes can break down plant fibre, it may seem strange that herbivores have not evolved the appropriate enzyme systems. The problem is that fibre is just too complex. It consists of a wide range of complex carbohydrates and associated compounds, notably hemicellulose, cellulose and lignin. These compounds are very different from each other and also each compound can vary considerably in different plants. Plants 'are not interested in being eaten' and 'use' the indigestibility of fibre (as well as a variety of other nasty compounds) as a protective mechanism. Apparently, kangaroos and ruminants are better served in combating the complexities of plant defences by relying on rapidly growing and changing cultures of micro-organisms.

The digestion of fibre is not the whole story of symbiosis. There are additional benefits to a kangaroo. The micro-organisms make vitamins and convert nitrogen-containing compounds into proteins which are utilised by the kangaroo. They also break down some potentially toxic substances that are in feed.

# GUT STRUCTURE

Fermentation can be a slow process and a large chamber must be provided to retain fibre long enough for sufficient digestion. Correct conditions also are needed to maintain high fermentation rates. These include precise levels of pH and electrolyte concentrations, which are largely provided via the saliva. Animals have evolved a variety of digestive systems to utilise fibre. The kangaroos have evolved a digestive system that has much in common with those found in ruminant mammals from other continents, but there are also unique features. The detail of gut function in kangaroos has been worked out only recently. Much of this understanding has come from Ian Hume and his students, notably Dave Dellow and David Freudenberger.

The basic structure of the kangaroo's gut is shown in Fig. 7.4 compared with the gut of the sheep and the horse. Kangaroos, like sheep, differ from horses in the way herbage is processed. Kangaroos and ruminants are known as 'forestomach fermenters', while horses and their relatives are 'hindgut fermenters'. The terms forestomach and hindgut relate to the position of the main fermentation chamber relative to the glandular, acid-secreting stomach and small intestine, which comprise the usual enzymatic digesting system.

There are advantages and disadvantages to both foregut and hindgut fermentation. They relate to the fact that, in addition to the fibre, plants have some cell contents that can be digested by normal enzymatic digestion. In the hindgut condition these cell contents are digested in the stomach and small intestine before reaching the fermentation chamber. Consequently, the horse does not have to pay 'microbial processing costs' on them. The fibre, however, passes through and is fermented in the voluminous colon. The disadvantage of this system is that some of the microbial population is lost in the faeces and, with it, valuable nutrients. With the forestomach system the microbes are digested by the glandular stomach and small intestine. However, the cell contents are also fermented along with the fibre in forestomachs, with subsequent loss of a portion of the easily available energy. The relative benefits of these two systems are determined by feed availability and the fibre content. The foregut system appears advantageous when fibre content is high, particularly if overall intake may be low. As well, the ruminants and kangaroos have additional fermentation capacity in the caecum and colon of their hindguts.

In sheep, plant material is kept in the sac-like rumen until it has been reduced to a small particle size. While this ensures a reasonable level of digestibility, problems can arise on very fibrous diets. Kangaroos seem to have a higher level of flexibility. Their forestomachs are largely tubular and this allows for a continuous throughput of material. The forestomach (Fig. 7.4 & Plate 16) is a spiral tubular organ with three main sections. The

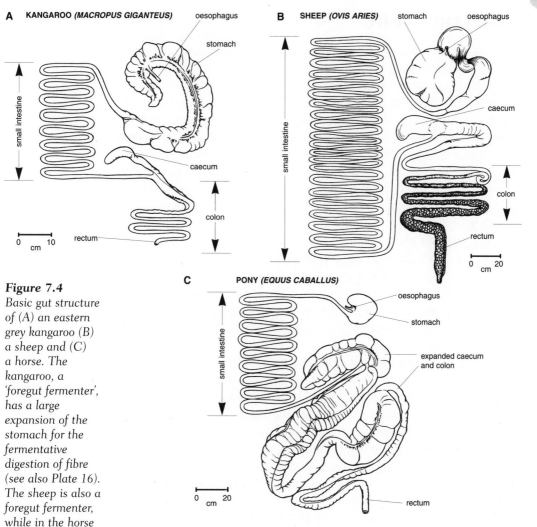

**A   KANGAROO *(MACROPUS GIGANTEUS)*** oesophagus

stomach

small intestine

caecum

colon

rectum

0   10
cm

**B   SHEEP *(OVIS ARIES)*** stomach   oesophagus

caecum

small intestine

colon

rectum

0   20
cm

**C   PONY *(EQUUS CABALLUS)*** oesophagus

stomach

expanded caecum
and colon

small intestine

0   20
cm

rectum

**Figure 7.4**
*Basic gut structure
of (A) an eastern
grey kangaroo (B)
a sheep and (C)
a horse. The
kangaroo, a
'foregut fermenter',
has a large
expansion of the
stomach for the
fermentative
digestion of fibre
(see also Plate 16).
The sheep is also a
foregut fermenter,
while in the horse
the fermentative
digestion of fibre
takes place in an
expanded caecum
and colon — the
horse is referred to
as a 'hindgut
fermenter. After
Stevens (1988).*

oesophagus admits food part-way along the tube, so that the initial segment
is a blind sac. This is called the sacciform forestomach and is S-shaped. In
some species of kangaroo the sacciform segment is separated from the large
coiled tubular section (tubiform forestomach) by a permanent fold, but this
is not obvious in the grey kangaroo. The tubiform section coils over and
then decreases in size to form the acid- and enzyme-secreting hind stomach. The pylorus is the opening into the small intestine.

The forestomach contents of kangaroos can be 9–10 per cent of total
body weight (Plate 16), against 14–15 per cent for sheep and goats; the
higher value for ruminants probably reflects their higher metabolic needs
(Chapter 8). These contents are some 70 per cent of the total fermentative
contents; the hindgut holds the rest. The small intestine of the kangaroos

is long and thin, though shorter than in sheep (Fig. 7.4). Of the large intestines, the caecum and proximal colon are of similar size to those of sheep. The distal colon and rectum are not as expanded as in sheep and it has been suggested that this is the reason that defaecation is more frequent in kangaroos.

Possible differences between kangaroos and sheep in the digestibility of fibre may be related to the structure of the gut and the rate of passage of the digesta. The movement of digesta in the gut of kangaroos is generally faster than that in sheep. In the kangaroo material from one period of feeding tends to move as a bolus through the large tubular forestomach and there is little mixing with previously ingested feed. As the material is moved along the forestomach it is subjected to microbial attack and there is progressive digestion of the food.

With the flow of digesta through a tubular forestomach it is possible to see where the digestion takes place. Dave Dellow and co-workers fed eastern grey kangaroos regularly to create a steady condition in the gut and then slaughtered them. The gut was divided into sections and the contents analysed. An indigestible and non-absorbable marker had been fed to the animal as well; this enabled calculation of the rates of nutrient digestion. With lucerne chaff 62 per cent of the organic matter was digested by fermentation in the forestomach. Virtually all of the soluble sugars were quickly removed, but fibre breakdown occurred gradually along the tubular forestomach. Only 33 per cent of fibre intake was digested in the forestomach but this was 85 per cent of the total digestion of this resistant fraction. The remainder of cellulose and lignin digestion occurs in the colon and caecum. Support for the finding that digestion in the forestomach of kangaroos occurs via fermentation is seen in the high levels of short-chain fatty acid production. There does not seem to be much protein digestion in the forestomach but proteins and other nitrogen-containing compounds are first processed into microbial protein, which is then digested in the intestine.

# FEED INTAKE

How much do kangaroos eat? This is not a simple question because there are differences in plant digestibility associated with fibre characteristics. Also, fibre digestion varies with body size. As animals get bigger they can maintain a larger fermenting stomach relative to their metabolic needs because metabolic rate does not increase directly with body size but at a slower rate (in proportion to the 0.75 power of body weight). This means that large kangaroos can retain feed longer in their forestomachs and increase its digestibility.

Feed intakes needed to provide maintenance requirements of nutrients have been determined for kangaroos eating chopped hay, usually good quality lucerne hay (Table 7.1). Such studies have often involved a comparison with sheep or goats. Maintenance (sustenance) intakes reflect the feed needed to just maintain the body weight of mature animals kept in small pens; that is, with low levels of activity.

**Table 7.1**

Representative values for the maintenance dry matter intakes of lucerne hay for average-sized kangaroos and ruminants held in pens

|  | Whole animal intake (g/day) | Digestibility of feed (%) |
|---|---|---|
| **Kangaroo (25 kg animal)** | | |
| Eastern grey(a) | 540 | 54 |
| Red | 590 | 55 |
| Euro | 610 | 59 |
| Wallaroo | 560 | 58 |
| **Ruminant (40 kg animal)** | | |
| Sheep | 1130 | 63 |
| Goat | 1020 | 65 |

(a) Values obtained for eastern grey kangaroos have been very variable; further investigation is needed.

Table 7.1 shows that there is little difference between kangaroo species in their basic maintenance requirements for feed and their ability to digest herbage. On lucerne hay the intakes of digestible dry matter are about 330 g per day for a 25 kg female (the most common age/size class). Maintenance intakes by sheep and goats are about double those of average-sized kangaroos, 690 g per day. Part of this difference is due to the bigger size of the ruminants compared to an average female kangaroo, and part is related to their higher energy needs; the basal metabolic rate of marsupials is 70 per cent of that of placentals.

The digestibility of plants by fermentation varies with their fibre structure and content, which influences both the rate and the absolute level of breakdown (Table 7.2). The stage of maturity of plants also affects their digestibility; note the differences shown in the table in rate and maximum level of digestion of young grass and mature dry grass. Consequently, the types of plant selected to be eaten will greatly influence the availability of nutrients to the kangaroo. Also, a kangaroo (or any herbivore) has to 'decide' whether to hold vegetation longer for more complete breakdown or to eat more and utilise only the rapidly fermented fraction. In drought, when availability is low and quality is poor, feed is retained in the gut for longer periods.

*Table 7.2*

Rates of fermentative digestion of dry matter in principal forage types (a)

| Forage type | Maximum dry matter digestion % | Digestion of dry matter after 4 hours % |
|---|---|---|
| Forbs, young (b) | 89 | 87 |
| Forbs, mature | 49 | 39 |
| Grass, young | 94 | 75 |
| Grass, mature dry | 57 | 15 |
| Shrubs, new leaves | 89 | 87 |
| Shrubs, woody twigs | 33 | 24 |

(a)  These results were obtained from samples suspended in nylon bags inside a goat rumen. Rates of digestion are similar in kangaroos.

(b)  Forbs are small herbaceous plants.

Intake of nutrients may be limited by stomach capacity if the feed contains too much water. Animals in the wild take account of this in their feeding strategies. Many forbs (small herbaceous plants) have high water content and are not preferred over grass unless they are more abundant. Species of kangaroo differ in the ability to handle 'soft' feed. Some red kangaroos I was keeping in yards lost weight on fresh young kikuyu grass and needed a supplement of dry pelleted feed. Eastern grey kangaroos easily maintained weight on the grass alone.

Actual patterns and levels of feed intake for red kangaroos and sheep have been determined in the wild by Steve McLeod, one of my PhD students. By detailed and painstaking observations he determined what plants, and which parts of those plants, were being eaten. By matching what was taken from plants in each bite by animals with similar-sized 'bites' he was able to build up a precise picture of the foraging of red kangaroos and sheep during different seasons. Such work is not glamorous. Crawling around in the dust at Fowlers Gap Station doing 'bite matching', or spending long periods at a telescope counting the number of bites a kangaroo takes in a feeding bout, may appear rather fanatical behaviour. However, this work has provided information and understanding which could not have been achieved otherwise.

The foraging patterns of an 'average' sheep (60 kg), male red kangaroo (60 kg) and female red kangaroo (25 kg) were determined during a good winter when there were plenty of growing forbs and during a summer drought when forbs were sparse and dry. As the season dried out there was a major shift, in the plants selected, from forbs and grass to grass and shrubs. Shrubs maintain growth longest into a drought. Grass became the major component of the diet of the smaller female red kangaroos in the dry conditions.

On the basis of the knowledge gained (from detailed observation and experiment) as to which parts of the plants are eaten, their water content and their digestibility, together with the rates at which the different plants were harvested, the total digestible dry matter intake was determined. This gave an idea of total energy intake. In the good winter red kangaroo males acquired 12,900 kJ/day, red kangaroo females 5700 kJ/day and sheep 17,500 kJ/day. During the hot dry summer the time available for foraging was restricted and intake and energy acquisition fell. For male red kangaroos energy intake was only 77 per cent of that in the good season, while for females it was 92 per cent and for sheep 93 per cent. Apart from subadults and young at foot, large male kangaroos appear the most susceptible of kangaroos to the ravages of drought.

## DIETS AND DIET PREFERENCES

What kangaroos eat has been of considerable interest because of concern on the part of pastoralists about competition between kangaroos and domestic stock. The simple reasoning was that, if kangaroos and domestic stock could eat similar feed, then the presence of kangaroos would reduce stock productivity. This can occur, but often in grazing country there is no competition, even though the diets overlap, because there is a surplus of feed for much of the time.

Recent studies of the diets of kangaroos and domestic stock in rangelands are now clarifying the situation regarding possible competition. Kangaroos of all species generally eat grasses and sedges (graminoids). This makes sense because the grasses are usually the most abundant ground vegetation and, if not too mature, they are reasonably digestible by kangaroos. However, kangaroos can eat a wide variety of vegetation, especially in hard times. For example, eastern grey kangaroos strip bark off eucalyptus trees during bad winters in the Australian Alps.

During a 12-year study at Fowlers Gap Station, which covered both very good seasons and severe droughts, Beverley Ellis and I recorded a wide range of diets for the mammalian herbivores. Most information was obtained for red kangaroos, euros and sheep and from the data distinct patterns of preference emerged (Table 7.3). The mix of plants that animals selected at a particular time was dependent on plant characteristics and relative availabilities. This in turn depended on rainfall, season, soil type, topography and past grazing pressure.

At times, guessing what any animal species is likely to be eating is easy. With good early summer rains young grass is abundant and it makes up most diets. It is nutritious and easily digested. This preference is seen in eastern and western grey kangaroos as well as red kangaroos and euros at Fowlers Gap. Green forbs may be abundant following winter and early

*Table 7.3*

Broad vegetation preferences of kangaroos and sheep at Fowlers Gap
Station in the far west of New South Wales

| Order of preference | Red kangaroos | Euros | Sheep |
|---|---|---|---|
| 1 | Young grass | Young grass | Green forbs |
| 2 | Green forbs | Mature grass | Young grass |
| 3 | Mature grass | Green forbs | Saltbush |
| 4 | Saltbush | Dry grass | Mature grass |
| 5 | Dry grass | Bluebush | Browse |
| 6 | Browse | Saltbush | Dry grass |
| 7 | Bluebush | Browse | Bluebush |

Saltbushes are salt-tolerant shrubs usually of the genus *Atriplex*
Bluebushes are salt-tolerant shrubs usually of the genus *Maireana*
Browse was mainly from trees of the genera *Acacia* and *Heterodendrum*

spring rain and then they can form a large part of the diets of sheep and
also of kangaroos. Some grasses, forbs and shrubs can be relatively unpalat-
able or even poisonous; such species tend to flourish as a result of overgrazing. Consequently, it is not *always* easy to guess diets from a quick look
at the vegetation. The palatability effects can be quite subtle. At Fowlers
Gap, for example, there are patches of soil with different acidity which support different bluebushes. On the more acid soil black bluebush largely
occurs and this is rarely eaten by euros. On the other hand, pearl bluebush,
which grows in less acid soil in parts of the hills, may form a significant part
of euro diets in dry times. Diets then can vary markedly over only hundreds
of metres for the sedentary euro.

# OVERLAP IN DIETS AND COMPETITION BETWEEN KANGAROO SPECIES

For competition to be demonstrated one species must have a deleterious
effect on another and this has yet to be shown between kangaroos. While
diet overlap has been reported for the different species of kangaroo in an
area, resource partitioning seems to exist. This occurs when species in an
area are eating different plant species within a group of plants and/or using
different parts of the habitat. Examples are described by Robert Taylor, who
studied eastern grey kangaroos and eastern wallaroos in the New England
region, and by David Croft, who studied antilopine kangaroos, northern
wallaroos and agile wallabies near Darwin. Generally euros and wallaroos

stand out from the other species because of their association with rough and hilly country. However, where euros do overlap in habitat with other species there can be a partial overlap in diets, usually in grass intake, and potential for competition exists.

Potential for competition exists between the two grey kangaroo species and between them and red kangaroos in semi-arid south-eastern Australia where all species occur together. Their diets overlap at times but the level of competition is uncertain. Eastern grey kangaroos and western grey kangaroos have differing microhabitat preferences, which in turn differ from those of red kangaroos. This is generally the case on Fowlers Gap Station, but not always. At times, all species can be seen feeding in the same area on the same plants.

# COMPETITION BETWEEN KANGAROOS AND SHEEP AND CATTLE

In the north of Australia the ground vegetation is dominated by grasses; for kangaroos and cattle these grasses comprise the bulk of their diets. While comparative diet studies have been made (see Dudzinski et al. 1982), no studies have looked for competitive interactions. Cattle and red kangaroos tend to eat different grasses or parts of grasses, as might be expected from the differences in size and structure of their teeth. There seems to be little overlap in the areas in which each species focuses its grazing, except in drought. Also, there is no evidence that kangaroos are attracted to areas where cattle crop down the vegetation. The general feeling is that the red kangaroos and cattle can coexist if cattle numbers are reasonably controlled. Dietary interactions between cattle and other species of kangaroo are largely unstudied.

The story of the interaction between kangaroos and sheep is more complex. Diet overlap between sheep and various species of kangaroo has been demonstrated a number of times. Whether *competition* occurs, and its nature if it does, have only recently received proper examination. Keep in mind the point that, for competition to be demonstrated, one species must have a deleterious effect on another.

The only study carried out under 'natural' conditions is Glen Edwards' PhD work with David Croft and me at Fowlers Gap Research Station. Six large paddocks (averaging 620 hectares each) with the same vegetation characteristics were divided into two paddocks with sheep and kangaroos, two with only kangaroos and two with only sheep. The kangaroos were largely kept out of the sheep-only paddocks by electric fences and regular culling of the few individuals that managed to get through these fences. Sheep were stocked at the usual rate for the district and the kangaroos were at their usual density; that is, at about the same density as the sheep.

While there was considerable overlap in diets between sheep and kangaroos, it was only during a very dry winter that competition occurred. Available vegetation on the ground was down to 45 g of plants (dried) per square metre. The sheep grazing with kangaroos changed their diet to include more saltbush, while those living without kangaroos maintained their intake of the more favoured grasses and forbs. At this time the sheep grazing in paddocks with kangaroos lost more weight and grew slightly less wool than the sheep in the paddocks free of kangaroos. These effects are seen as competitive effects of kangaroos on sheep, with the presence of kangaroos reducing the grass availability to sheep.

Competition was not one-sided, however. Although the presence of sheep in this dry time did not influence kangaroo diets, the kangaroos which grazed with sheep had lower body weights than those in the sheep-free paddocks. The kangaroos that were most affected were older males and small females. Other studies show that these are classes which have high mortality in droughts.

The study could not examine severe drought because one did not occur for several years. Information from earlier diet studies of all the mammalian herbivores at Fowlers Gap Station did cover such a period. In early 1983 plant availability dropped below 10 g (dry mass) per square metre. Overlap in diets between sheep and red kangaroos on the plains country was large, 87 per cent. Since mortality was significant in both red kangaroos and sheep and since wool production per sheep was significantly depressed, it can be expected that each species would have been better off if the other had not been present — that is, severe competition probably occurred. Interestingly, in the hill country of the Station sheep and euros did not have such a level of diet overlap. There was much more saltbush in this area and the sheep maintained themselves largely on this. The euros tried to maintain themselves on the almost non-existent grasses and suffered a major population crash. If the saltbush had been eaten out, as has happened through sheep-grazing over much of the arid rangelands, the Station sheep would have been similarly affected.

Where other species of kangaroo are concerned, it is likely that they will come into competition for feed with domestic animals in dry to drought times. The characteristics of that competition will vary with the nature of the vegetation and with the animal species and their number. A handful of kangaroos will not compete significantly with hundreds of sheep in a paddock, but the sheep will impact on the kangaroos. For the sheep, in such a situation, intraspecies competition (level of stocking) would be the dominant factor in their well-being.

A question that has not been resolved relates to the impact of kangaroos on 'spelled' paddocks: paddocks from which sheep are removed to allow the land to recover from overgrazing. There are suggestions that such paddocks fail to recover because kangaroos move in and utilise any vegetation. A comment often made by graziers is: 'It is no use spelling paddocks because it only feeds the kangaroos'. Work at Fowlers Gap has shown that if areas are not overgrazed the presence or absence of sheep does not affect kangaroo distribution. However, an overgrazed area would be expected to have a small number of kangaroos and as it improved the population could build up to normal levels. Another side of this story relates to responses after rain. Rain on degraded areas can quickly produce new green growth of a transient nature. Kangaroos, particularly young mobile animals, may move onto this ephemeral feed in numbers. But their overall impact on the long-term carrying capacity of such land is unknown. Degraded areas may be eroded and reduced in fertility, so that reasonable recovery of the vegetation is just not possible in the short term.

# LIVING IN THE ENVIRONMENT — ENVIRONMENTAL PHYSIOLOGY

## METABOLIC LEVELS

As a general characteristic, kangaroos have basal metabolic rates that are about 70 per cent of those of comparable placental mammals. The basal metabolic rate is the idling speed of an animal, to use the analogy of a car engine. It reflects the minimum energy turnover of resting animals that have not eaten recently and are in a thermally comfortable environment. Because large animals such as kangaroos normally spend a lot of time resting, the level of basal metabolism impacts on many aspects of their physiology. As seen in Chapter 7, the energy intakes of grazing red kangaroos are lower than those of sheep. Ken Nagy and co-workers obtained similar results when examining the field metabolic rates of eastern grey kangaroos and black-tailed deer. Water use and protein requirements are other systems in which differences are seen between kangaroos and placental equivalents.

While a relatively low basal metabolism impacts on a kangaroo's physiology this does not mean that kangaroos are not energetic animals — quite the contrary. Kangaroos, like other marsupials, are potentially very energetic animals. Our insights into this come largely from looking at their locomotion, which relates to predator avoidance and the ability to move long distances rapidly to find feed and water. Also, energetic capability may play a role in the extended fighting of males. The notion of kangaroos being an athletic species is recent, though it should have been obvious all along. Kangaroos can outrun dogs and horses — and these are among the most athletic of placental mammals. True, kangaroos have an energetically efficient, specialised form of locomotion, but hopping may have evolved *because* marsupials had the inherent high energetic ability to capitalise on it. While hopping is energetically efficient, to sustain it at high speed still requires a lot of energy. Indirect evidence further supports the idea of a high metabolic capability: kangaroos have hearts one-third bigger than those of comparable placentals; and, per breath, kangaroos can move relatively much more air through their lungs.

To date we have only a sketchy idea of the costs of activities in the wild because of the difficulty in obtaining such information. Insights are available from work with kangaroos kept in a small paddock at Fowlers Gap Research Station. With the aid of students and Earthwatch volunteers, I monitored the behaviour of red kangaroos in an eight-hectare paddock with good natural feed. I assessed the animals' metabolism via heart rate measurements made with implanted radio telemetry units. Energy use for females was some 4000 kJ/day in summer. There was a higher cost in winter, 5000 kJ/day, due to the cold nights. These values are slightly lower than those estimated from Steve McLeod's foraging studies, possibly because the enclosed kangaroos in my study were less active.

The relative costs of some behaviours were also established. Taking the cost of sleeping in the sun as a base, the cost of lying alert was 20 per cent more; for standing it was 30 per cent more; for feeding quietly it was 45 per cent more and for slow walking it was 90 per cent more. We did not get measures for continuous hopping (the paddock was relatively small) but hopping on a treadmill required a 2000 per cent increase! Given these results it is obvious that the overall cost of the daily activities of a kangaroo will be strongly influenced by how much travelling (hopping) it does. Red kangaroos can travel 10 km to and from water. They can do this quickly, perhaps an hour or so in travelling time, but such a trip would almost double the energy use for that day (it's like a human running in a half-marathon). In a dry summer when feed is scarce such a trip would be a major burden. No wonder red kangaroos drink infrequently! At Fowlers Gap we have noted that those animals that drink most frequently live close to a water point.

# TEMPERATURE REGULATION — BEHAVIOURAL ASPECTS

Kangaroos, like most marsupials, try to maintain their core body temperature near 36°C, slightly lower than most placental mammals. When faced with a thermally challenging environment the first thing that kangaroos do is to try to avoid it. This is not just for reasons of comfort. In cold conditions, maintaining body temperature (keeping warm) can require considerable metabolic heat and that means more food. Renata Jaremovic recorded mass mortality in young eastern grey kangaroos when there was a combination of poor feed supplies and cold wet winters in the southern tablelands of New South Wales.

When the weather is hot, water becomes a limiting factor. Once environmental temperature nears, or goes above, body temperature a kangaroo can prevent overheating (keep cool) only by the evaporation of water. Travelling to water is energetically costly and cuts down on feeding time; also most predation occurs at waterholes. With an understanding of these factors it is easy to see that behaviour which reduces the impact of hot or cold conditions can be very beneficial.

What are the environmental conditions that kangaroos need to avoid? Animals gain or lose heat by radiation, conduction and convection, and exchange of heat with their surroundings in these ways largely depends on the temperature differences. In a cold environment kangaroos lose heat in proportion to the coldness of the environment, and the reverse happens in hot conditions. The simplest thing that a kangaroo can do to reduce environmental stress is to find a more moderate microenvironment. Euros' use of cool caves in summer is an obvious example.

The thermal environment in nature is complex. The sun has a major impact via solar radiation. At midday in summer at Fowlers Gap Station the potential heat load from solar radiation is 1000 Watts/m². A kangaroo lying down exposes a surface of about 0.5 m², so, in the sun, 500 Watts would reach it. If all this was absorbed as heat the kangaroo would have to evaporate almost 4.5 litres of water per hour to get rid of it. Obviously, not all the heat is absorbed because of the characteristics of the fur, but avoiding the sun on hot days saves a lot of water. Conversely, in winter it can pay, energetically, to move into the sun. On a cold winter's morning any solar radiation absorbed means less feed has to be found. Sun-seeking is often observed among kangaroos in the colder parts of Australia.

Another major source of radiation heat exchange is the sky. The atmosphere is a complex mixture of gases, dust, smoke and clouds. Some of its components, such as water vapour, carbon dioxide, dust and smoke particles, absorb radiation (heat) at the wavelengths given off by animals and the earth generally, so this heat is not lost to outer space. Such absorbed radiation is partially radiated back to the earth; this is the greenhouse effect. During the day solar radiation, direct and scattered, results in the radiation temperature of the sky being close to air temperature. However, at night and in the early morning and late afternoon the effective sky temperature falls, particularly if the amount of water, carbon dioxide and smoke is low.

**Figure 8.1**
*Behavioural responses to thermal extremes save water and energy. Euros make use of caves, a mild microhabitat, to avoid the extremes of a desert summer day.*

Such conditions are notable in deserts and during winter in regions away from the coast. Desert kangaroos make use of the 'heat sink' of the sky to lose heat in summer from late afternoon into the evening, even though air temperatures may still be high. Eastern grey kangaroos keep in the shelter of trees and scrub on cold clear winter nights to screen themselves from this heat sink.

Wind is another obvious climatic factor that impacts on thermoregulation. Kangaroos can avoid wind or make use of its effects. Wind is a problem in cold conditions because it disrupts the insulation provided by the animal's fur. The stronger the wind the greater the breakdown in insulation. Eastern grey kangaroos shelter during cold windy nights. Their winter pelts are also noticeably thicker in the colder parts of their range. Red kangaroos at Fowlers Gap Station also stop foraging during the coldest times of windy winter nights and shelter behind shrubs and bushes. They may even move their home-ranges off the plains and into hilly country for more shelter when the winter westerlies are blowing.

All species of kangaroo use behavioural means to reduce thermal stress, but this tendency shows up most clearly in desert species. Martin Denny and I have studied the behavioural adjustments made by euros and red kangaroos during hot summer days. These species can live in the same area but they differ in their behaviour. The euro is much more the 'avoider'. It hides away from the heat in small caves and rock overhangs. This microhabitat cuts out any significant solar radiation (Fig 8.1). Also, the walls of caves are relatively cool. The rock mass surrounding caves hardly changes in temperature during the day; it changes less than 10°C throughout the year. In one cave that we examined, air temperature at midday was 10°C below the outside air temperature. The radiation status of the cave walls was such that a euro could lose heat via this route, as compared to the large potential heat *gain* of a red kangaroo resting under a small mulga tree. Some caves and rock overhangs are smaller and more open than others and the air temperature is closer to that outside. How do euros cope in these stuffy spaces with little air movement? I certainly felt hot and sweaty crawling in them. The difference for the euro is that it pants in order to evaporate water and to cool itself. By panting it moves air over the body surfaces from which evaporation occurs; it does not have to rely on wind to increase evaporation rates as do humans, who primarily *sweat*. More about this in a moment.

Red kangaroos in the open country are in a very different situation. Their only protection from solar radiation is sparse desert trees; but these screen out over three-quarters of incoming radiation. Red kangaroos spend much time lying quietly in this shade. In early afternoon on hot clear days greater avoidance of sunlight is needed and the animals adopt a particular stance. They stand crouched in the shade with their tails pulled between their legs (Fig. 8.2). This posture provides the smallest surface for radiant heat inflow. The kangaroo's fur provides further protection. About 30 per cent of incoming radiation is reflected; that which is absorbed ends up as heat at the fur surface. Most of this surface heat does not pass into the kangaroo's body but is convected away in the air if there is wind. All in all, little of the sun's radiation heat load gets through to a red kangaroo if it stays in the shade.

**Figure 8.2**
*On the open plains red kangaroos use the shade of a small desert tree to reduce the heat load from solar radiation. Even such shade can reduce incoming solar radiation by 80 per cent. Note the 'hunched' stance with the tail pulled between the legs to further minimise the area exposed to the sun.*

# TEMPERATURE REGULATION — PHYSIOLOGICAL THERMOREGULATION

*Figure 8.3*

*Influence of air temperatures on body temperature, heat production during summer and winter and evaporative heat loss in red kangaroos. Body temperature varies little over a large range of air temperatures. Increased fur insulation in winter reduces the need for extra heat production to maintain body temperature at low air temperatures. At high air temperatures body heat can be lost only via the evaporation of water. After Dawson (1989).*

Maintenance of a relatively stable body temperature relies on the ability to produce sufficient heat in the cold and to get rid of heat in hot conditions. Of course, a control system to manage the heat balance of the body is also needed. In mammals the controlling system is centred in the floor of the brain — in the hypothalamus. This is where the reference temperature, the setting of the body's thermostat, is determined and where the multitude of sensors placed throughout the body send their information about its thermal status.

It is a highly complex system but its main feature is that it anticipates potential changes and makes precautionary adjustments. For example, if conditions alter in a way that favours significant heat loss (e.g. if rain occurs on a cold day) thermal sensors in the skin pick up changes at the surface before there is any change in deep body temperatures. The system then takes action to reduce overall heat loss, such as by changing the blood flow to the skin, and if necessary to start producing extra heat through shivering (see below). In all but extreme conditions these anticipatory responses by the controller in the brain limit changes in deep body temperatures.

## RESPONSES TO COLD

The major physiological responses to cold are increased insulation and increased heat production. Initially, as the air temperature decreases below the warm comfortable zone, a kangaroo increases its body insulation. This is not done by changing fur insulation. Heat loss is largely adjusted by changing patterns of blood flow in the legs and tail. The aim is to stop heat being carried from the body core via the blood to surfaces where it can be lost. A point can be reached where the kangaroo cannot maintain body temperature by such vascular adjustments (Fig. 8.3) and extra heat has to be produced. Kangaroos do this by shivering. The rate of shivering is dependent on the difference between body and air temperatures.

Fur does influence the overall rate of heat loss. In winter kangaroos 'put on their winter coat', and for red kangaroos (Fig. 8.3) this makes a large difference in the need to produce extra heat when it gets cold. Graham Brown

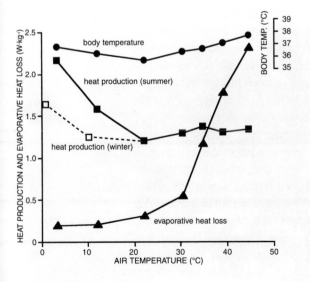

of CSIRO and I found that red kangaroos had relatively low fur insulation in summer but doubled it in winter, which reflects the seasonal temperature extremes in the desert. Eastern grey kangaroos from the southern highlands of Australia carry heavy fur insulation most of the time, while the tropical antilopine kangaroo has low insulation throughout the year; its physiology concentrates on heat loss.

## THERMOREGULATION IN THE HEAT

In moderate environments, 20–32°C, kangaroos maintain a stable body temperature by fine changes in blood flow to adjust whole body insulation. As environmental temperature rises toward body temperature at 36°C the gradient for heat loss by radiation, conduction and convection diminishes and, even with marked blood flow to the body surface, sufficient heat cannot be lost without resorting to the evaporation of water. The evaporation of one millilitre of water requires 2.43 kJ of heat. Since air has a very low heat-holding capacity, if water is evaporated at a body surface then almost all the heat comes from the kangaroo. When the environmental temperature is equal to body temperature all heat has to be lost by the evaporation of water. Additionally, if environmental temperature, which may include a solar radiation heat load, exceeds body temperature, then heat can flow into the body and this heat will also have to be lost by the evaporation of water.

In hot environments any extra activity or exercise generates more heat that has to be dissipated by the evaporation of water. If exercise is substantial then even in cool environments evaporation is also needed to allow adequate heat loss. This is especially true with kangaroos and other 'athletic' mammals such as horses. They have to be able to dump the heat or they have to stop producing it; that is, slow down or stop exercising.

Kangaroos have elaborate evaporative heat loss mechanisms. The various species all seem to have these abilities. I have worked with the desert red kangaroos and they are without equal among mammals when it comes to dissipating heat. This is the case whether the heat originates from the environment or from internal production as a result of exercise. Three mechanisms of evaporative heat loss are used: panting, sweating and licking.

Panting is the main route of evaporative heat loss in resting red kangaroos. Panting is rapid shallow breathing in which the air movement over the nasal passages and upper respiratory tract is greatly increased. During panting the respiration rate may exceed 300 breaths per minute. Air movement deep in the lungs is not altered, however, and normal exchange of oxygen and carbon dioxide is not disturbed until extreme conditions occur. The rate of evaporation, and therefore heat loss, is adjusted by varying the air flow over, and the blood flow to, the upper airways. Since the body's heat is lost from a small area the flow of blood, which carries the heat, has to be high. An increase of 66 times in blood flow to the nasal surfaces from

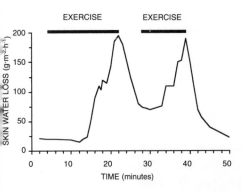

**Figure 8.4**
*Sweating in a red kangaroo in response to exercise. Sweating in kangaroos is an auxiliary evaporative heat loss mechanism. It ceases when exercise stops and the kangaroo relies on water-efficient panting, with licking, to drop body temperature to normal. After Dawson, Robertshaw and Taylor (1974).*

cool to hot conditions has been measured in red kangaroos.

Kangaroos do sweat also. During sweating evaporation occurs at the skin, which is kept cooler than the body core. Heat is rapidly transported in the blood to sparsely furred skin for dissipation. This is effective, but in hot sunny environments the maintenance of a cool skin increases heat inflow. Such heat has to be immediately lost from the skin and this requires much extra water. This is not a problem if water is plentiful, but this is not always so in Australia and therefore panting has advantages. Exercise, however, produces much heat. Hopping results in heat being produced at more than 25 times the basal metabolic rate. Considerable heat is still lost from the respiratory tract in these circumstances, as ventilation is greatly increased to provide extra oxygen, but the respiratory system cannot handle the whole heat load. Sweating is then utilised as an auxiliary evaporative heat loss mechanism. Hopping in hot environments really places a strain on heat loss mechanisms. Some other large mammals, such as horses, use sweating but a unique feature of kangaroos is that sweating stops as soon as exercise ceases (Fig. 8.4.). This is true even when body temperature is still elevated and the animal is still panting rapidly. The advantage of switching off sweating and then relying on panting is related to economy in water use.

The third route of evaporative heat loss is licking, which is also used by kangaroos. This is, in fact, the most easily observed response of the various kangaroos to high temperatures. During a bout of licking, 'saliva' that has dripped from the mouth is wiped or licked on the forearms; the tongue is not necessarily involved. Our attitudes to the importance of licking have changed over the years. Until 30 years ago kangaroos were considered primitive and inferior in their thermoregulatory abilities. Licking was considered an 'early evolutionary step' in the development of heat loss and the fact that kangaroos licked themselves simply reinforced the notions about their primitiveness. In retrospect such ideas had no support, but even when we began to understand the superior abilities of kangaroos the role of licking was a puzzle. The problem was that the area licked was small and it was hard to imagine how it could play a significant role in heat loss. The problem was solved when Alan Needham and I found that in the region of the forearm licked by the red kangaroo there is a dense superficial network of fine blood vessels (Fig. 8.5). In collaboration with Bob Hales, then of CSIRO, we showed that there were marked increases in blood flow through the foreleg in warm and hot conditions, so significant heat loss was possible.

The water for licking comes from water-secreting glands in the nose and from the salivary glands. Under heat stress these various glands tend to

**Figure 8.5**
*Network of superficial blood vessels under the forelimb skin of a red kangaroo. These vessels lie just under the area that is 'licked', and a high blood flow indicates that they are involved in significant heat loss.*

overproduce in order to make sure the ventilated air is fully saturated — much in the way that sweat glands can overproduce. The water is spread on an area where the fur is thin and where high blood flow is provided. In this way all water is used for thermoregulation. A further point that I have only just appreciated is that the area of the forearms that is licked is protected from solar radiation by the stance of the body. Licking an area that was fully exposed to the sun would be a waste of effort. Antilopine kangaroos in the tropics lick the insides of their legs (similarly shielded) and this region is highly vascularised. Males of all species also lick their scrotal region in the heat.

This array of characteristics makes the red kangaroo among the most heat-tolerant of mammals — a level of tolerance achieved with minimal water use. The thermoregulatory abilities of other species of kangaroo are not so well understood. The grey kangaroos have not been studied in detail but they do show some differences from the other species. At Fowlers Gap in hot weather eastern grey kangaroos had daily body temperature fluctuations that were much larger than those of red kangaroos (Fig. 8.6). The eastern greys maintained significantly lower body temperatures during the hottest part of the day and would face a larger gradient for heat flow into the body. From their frequency of drinking it appears they are not as economical in their water use as the red kangaroos are.

**Figure 8.6**
*Telemetrically recorded deep body temperatures of red kangaroos and eastern grey kangaroos at Fowlers Gap Station in summer (air temperatures are shown above). The body temperatures of the grey kangaroos varied much more and their frequency of drinking was much greater. Sunrise and sunset are indicated respectively by open and filled arrows. After McCarron and Dawson(1989).*

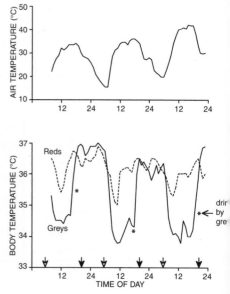

# WATER RELATIONS

In the early 1970s I spent two summers with Martin Denny, Eleanor Russell and Beverley Ellis at Fowlers Gap Research Station studying the water relations of free-ranging red kangaroos, euros, sheep and feral goats. I still look back at that time and wonder at our enthusiasm. As usual, the story was a little complex but the important findings were that the two species of kangaroo used (turned over) much less water (Fig. 8.7) and drank much less often than the sheep and goats did.

Drinking frequencies through summer were very different. The sheep were watering daily and twice a day on hot days (over 30–35°C maximum), while the feral goats seemed to drink every second day. Kangaroos drank at irregular intervals; the peak number of returns to water for both red kangaroos and euros was at five days, with almost none returning before three nights had passed. However, many kangaroos of both species had longer periods between drinks even in hot weather. We collared 50 red kangaroos and 100 euros over a period of about two weeks and then monitored the water trap for a further 12 days — so all animals had a chance to return within 12 days. Just half of the red kangaroos returned for a drink within 12 days of collaring, while only a third of the euros did so. I consider that these different drinking frequencies mostly reflect the microhabitat selection of the euros, but differences in physiology are also involved.

Field water use has not been studied in all kangaroo species. Both species of grey kangaroo do drink more frequently in summer than the red kangaroos and euros. Early work done by Graeme Caughley in south-west Queensland, in which he counted the faecal pellet deposition near water, indicated that eastern grey kangaroos visited water three times as often as red kangaroos. This pattern of high water use by grey kangaroos is supported by yard and laboratory studies. When faced with water shortage the eastern grey kangaroos dehydrate more quickly than red kangaroos and euros. The ready access to stock watering points probably explains why the grey kangaroos have moved into drier country in the last half-century.

**Figure 8.7**
*Water use (turnover) by red kangaroos, euros, feral goats and sheep during summer at Fowlers Gap Station. The turnover, in millilitres of water per kilogram of body weight per day, represents water obtained from food in addition to that from drinking. Derived from Dawson et al. (1975).*

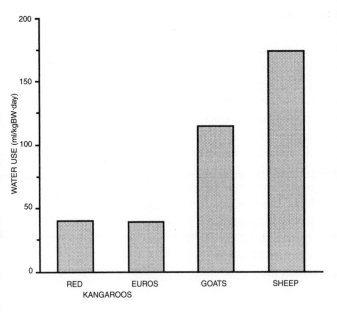

# WATER BALANCE OF KANGAROOS

About 75 per cent by weight of a kangaroo's body is water, which is a high proportion compared to most mammals. The reason for this is twofold. Wild mammals such as kangaroos carry little fat; fat has a much lower water content than muscle has. Sheep and goats in good 'condition' have body water contents of near 65 per cent. The large foregut and extended caeca of kangaroos also contain considerable water. It has often been suggested that the rumen or the forestomach could act as a large store of water that could be used in an emergency. However, the water content of these fermentative chambers needs to be kept above 82–85 per cent for effective functioning. Decreases in the gut water volume in red kangaroos and euros have been noted during dehydration, but work done by David Freudenberger on euros and goats suggests that such decreases in gut water volume are due to an overall decline in gut contents and not just water. This means that feed intake has been reduced.

Kangaroos can withstand losses of body water that would be fatal to a human. We are seriously debilitated and may suffer circulatory collapse when water equivalent to 12 per cent of our body weight is lost, while red kangaroos and euros appear unaffected by losses above 20 per cent of body weight. They recover such losses almost totally within 24 hours when drinking water is provided; about half the water can be replaced within five minutes. Although Martin Denny and I found that the pattern of water loss throughout the body differed between red kangaroos and euros, a feature of both species was the maintenance of blood volume. This was not seen in eastern grey kangaroos examined by Hugh McCarron.

The water balance of kangaroos is just that, a balance between inputs and outputs. Obviously, both inputs and outputs can change in different environmental situations. An example of such changes appeared in work done by Martin Denny and me on red kangaroos.

We habituated kangaroos to life in special metabolism cages so that all faeces and urine could be collected and water and feed intakes measured. We found that in the cool conditions the water use of red kangaroos was about 40 ml/kg.day (Fig. 8.8). Water loss in the faeces (43 per cent) was the main route of water loss, while losses in the urine and as uncontrolled insensible evaporation were similar. Drinking water formed 72 per cent of water intake; with water in food, followed by water produced during metabolism, making up the total water added to the body. The feed was dry, less than 20 per cent water; but if it had been fresh grass then water balance could have been maintained without drinking. For six to eight of the cooler months of the year red kangaroos rarely drink if good green feed is available.

If drinking water is scarce in droughts red kangaroos conserve water by concentrating their urine (up to 4.1 osmol/kg) and producing much drier

**Figure 8.8**
*Water balance of red kangaroos in different circumstances on relatively dry feed. In moderate conditions faeces is the main route of water loss. In the absence of drinking water kangaroos cut food intake, thereby reducing faecal losses, and further maximise water savings by producing drier faeces and more concentrated urine. By eating green feed they could be in water balance. In hot conditions the kangaroos replace water used in temperature regulation by drinking; even with green feed and full water conservation they need to drink. Unpublished data of M.J.S. Denny and T.J. Dawson.*

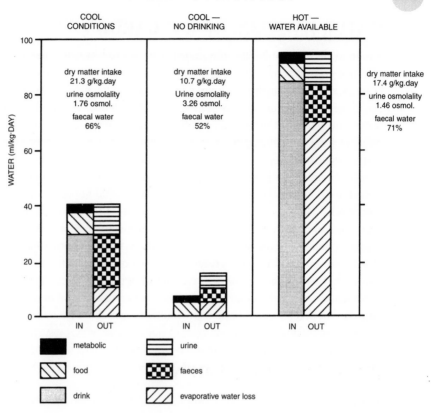

faeces. Basically, they reduce the amount of water used in the excretion of their waste products. This may not be sufficient to bring them into water balance even in winter if moist feed is unavailable. However, a major benefit of being able to produce concentrated urine occurs if succulent, but salty, desert shrubs such as saltbush (*Atriplex* spp.) are available. The kangaroos are able to eat such shrubs and have a net water gain. This may occur also if they drink the saline water that commonly occurs in lakes and springs throughout the inland. The effect is similar to the situation of marine mammals which have good concentrating kidneys and achieve a net water gain from taking in seawater because they can excrete the salt with less water than they drank. The abilities of red kangaroos in this regard are seen in dry times at Fowlers Gap Station, when both they and sheep turn to eating saltbush. The sheep start drinking more frequently than the kangaroos do and have to forage closer to the water point where feed is poorer.

In experimentally simulated hot summer conditions the water use of red kangaroos rose markedly to 95 ml/kg. day (Fig. 8.8). This was due solely to increased evaporative loss for thermoregulation; water loss by other routes did not change. The kangaroos did not increase water conservation tactics. The increased evaporative loss was simply balanced by increased drinking.

How frequently each kangaroo species has to drink in hot weather will depend largely on how it limits this thermoregulatory water use.

On balance, there is little difference between red kangaroos and euros in water conservation. Red kangaroos can produce a more concentrated urine, 4.1 osmol/kg against 3.3 osmol/kg for euros. However, euros produce drier faeces. Dehydrated euros produce faeces with only about 42 per cent water; this is about the minimum value seen in mammals. The major differences between these species in water relations lie in their thermoregulatory response to heat.

In comparison with red kangaroos and euros, both species of grey kangaroo have relatively high water use in warm to hot conditions but as yet we do not have an explanation for this. Water use in euros and wallaroos has been studied in more detail. These subspecies resemble each other in patterns of water use, with some minor differences. Euros can produce faeces about 10 per cent drier than eastern wallaroos can; David Freudenberger attributed this to the euro having a colon 30 per cent longer than that of the wallaroo. Water is removed from the faeces in the colon and rectum. Of note, the red kangaroo has a significantly longer colon than the eastern grey kangaroo does.

# PROTEIN REQUIREMENTS

Energy and water requirements influence the distributions of the various species of kangaroo but whether protein has a role in this regard is unknown. Protein needs are usually determined as the minimum amount needed to maintain a steady protein level in the body. It is often determined as 'daily nitrogen maintenance requirement', since nitrogen is a distinctive and consistent component (16%) of the amino acids that make up protein. Actually, with kangaroos and ruminants, nitrogen requirement is an appropriate description because in these forestomach fermenters virtually any nitrogen that enters that gut is incorporated into microbial protein. This microbial protein is later digested further down the digestive tract.

The basic pattern is that kangaroos have maintenance requirements for protein which are about 20–30 per cent lower than grazing placentals of similar size. This is probably related to the lower metabolic rate of the kangaroos. There is some variation among the kangaroos; estimates for the eastern grey kangaroos, eastern wallaroos and euros are respectively 24, 25 and 20 grams of protein per day for 25 kg animals. With such a low requirement the euro appears specially adapted to forage on feed of low protein content. In the Pilbara district of Western Australia the availability of nitrogen in the spinifex grass is so low that sheep restrict their reproduction. But euros in this environment readily cope with reproduction, in which there is a major demand for protein for the tissues of the growing young.

That some kangaroo species may be nitrogen-deficient in some environments has been suggested but never demonstrated. Generally, energy intake is considered the most important aspect of nutrition. Kangaroos (and ruminants) have special nitrogen-conserving mechanisms that can be brought into play. The mechanism is called nitrogen, or urea, recycling.

Urea is a nitrogen-containing waste product derived from the breakdown and turnover of proteins. It is largely produced in the liver and excreted via the kidney. If nitrogen intake is low, instead of being excreted the urea is reabsorbed in its passage through the kidney and ends up back in the blood leaving the kidney. This urea is secreted into the saliva and travels back into the forestomach to be turned into usable microbial protein. Some urea also enters the forestomach directly from the blood bathing its walls.

Not all the nitrogen that is processed by the kidneys can be reclaimed and some is lost in the faeces. However, this process of recycling the waste urea back into available microbial protein obviously means, for kangaroos, that their protein requirements in feed are much reduced. The recycling of urea also has additional benefits to kangaroos in arid conditions. If urea is recycled then water does not have to be made available for its excretion and this results in significant reductions in urinary water loss.

## CHAPTER 9

# KANGAROOS AND HUMANS — ABORIGINES

The first encounters between Aboriginal people and kangaroos are truly 'lost in the mists of time' — unlike the discovery of kangaroos by Europeans. Australia has been an island for the last million years or so, during which time the modern human evolved. While humans inhabited South-east Asia, including the Indonesian islands, during this time, just when they entered Australia is uncertain. The current best estimates are between 40,000 and 60,000 years ago. The uncertainty exists because there is little available archaeological material and the speculated time of arrival is just beyond the limit of accurate dating using the $^{14}$C radioactive isotope of carbon. Reliable radiocarbon dates indicate that Aborigines were established in the Murray–Darling River basin around 35,000 years ago, so presumably they were also spread throughout mainland Australia at that time.

## GIANT KANGAROOS AND THE MEGAFAUNA

Whenever the Aborigines arrived they must have been even more astounded by the mammals they encountered than were the Europeans later on. At that early time the mammalian fauna was much more diverse and included many large or giant species. This assemblage of large species is generally referred to as 'megafauna'; it included kangaroos and other

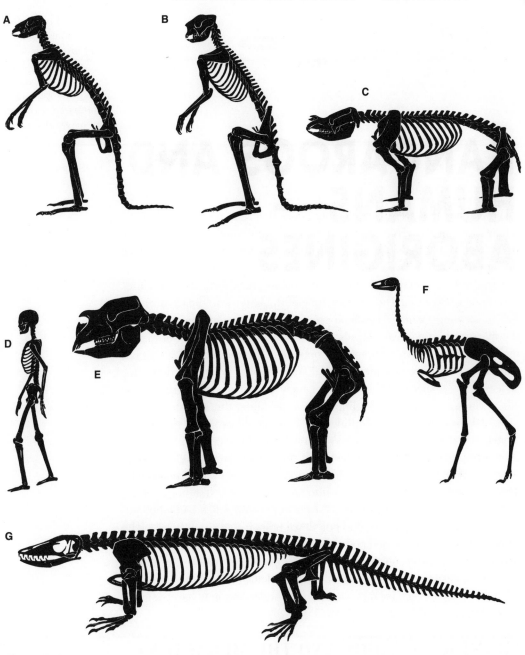

**Figure 9.1**

*Skeletal restorations of some Australian Pleistocene megafauna showing the probable size relationships of the biggest 'kangaroos' to other forms: (A) the giant ancestor of the eastern grey kangaroo (Macropus titan); (B) the largest sthenurine 'kangaroo' (Procoptodon goliah); (C) marsupial 'rhinoceros' (Zygomaturus trilobus); (D) human — the skeleton represents someone 177 cm tall and weighing 80kg; (E) the largest marsupial to have lived (Diprotodon optatum); (F) a bird much larger than an emu (Genyornis newtoni); (G) giant goanna (Megalania prisca). After Murray (1991).*

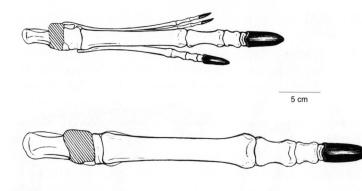

5 cm

**Figure 9.2**
*The foot structure
of an extinct large
macropodine
kangaroo,*
Macropus titan,
*compared with that
of an extinct 'giant'
sthenurine
'kangaroo',*
Procoptodon goliah.
*After Murray
(1991).*

macropodines that were considerably larger than any now alive. A wide-ranging examination of the megafauna and the role of Aborigines in its extinction has recently been provided by Peter Murray of the Alice Springs Museum.

Large size was not restricted to the mammals; there were also giant birds and reptiles (Fig. 9.1). The most exciting of the latter would have been the 4–5 metre long goanna, *Megalania prisca*. The spectacular mammals were the marsupial 'rhinoceros', *Zygomaturus trilobus*, and the largest of marsupials, the giant browser *Diprotodon optatum*. The megafaunal kangaroos and their relatives represented a broad and complex radiation, comprising at least 20–30 species. These came largely from two major groups, the sthenurines and the macropodines, the latter being the ancestors of our present kangaroos. The sthenurines are now totally extinct. They were a large group of browsing 'kangaroos', characterised by short deep skulls and even more specialised hopping feet than the modern macropodine kangaroos have (Fig. 9.2). The largest of the sthenurines was *Procoptodon goliah*. This was probably the largest 'kangaroo' to have existed, standing over 2.5 metres tall and weighing perhaps 200 kg. *Procoptodon goliah* had long forelimbs that may have been used to pull down branches to reach foliage. The largest of the 'true' (macropodine) kangaroos were *Macropus ferragus*, which was a giant euro/wallaroo, and *Macropus titan*, which was a giant form of the eastern grey kangaroo. While these kangaroos probably stood as tall as *Procoptodon goliah*, they were more slender and may have weighed about 150 kg.

## Megafaunal extinction

Why don't these spectacular kangaroos still exist? A simple, and possibly true, answer is that the Aborigines ate them. Big animals tend to be slow and they provide a lot of meat. If this were the case, it would fit with a pattern often seen throughout the world when naive populations of animals are first confronted with a new, highly efficient predator, such as the human. This has happened in the Americas, Eurasia and New Zealand.

Scientists and anthropologists tend to suspect simple explanations and the causes of the megafaunal extinction in Australia are still vigorously debated. Part of the reason for this debate is the notion that Aboriginal people lived in complete balance and harmony with the environment. Most ecologists find this concept naive. Still, direct evidence that Aborigines caused these extinctions (i.e. 'kill sites') is limited and alternative explanations have been suggested, such as marked climate change. It is also suggested that Aboriginal use of fire may have caused extinctions by grossly modifying the environment to the detriment of the large vertebrates.

Climate change alone can be dismissed as the sole cause of the extinction of the large kangaroos and associated fauna. True, there was a marked period of severe aridity in the late Pleistocene. This was associated with the last great ice age when much water was locked up in expanded polar ice sheets. The sea level fell so much that the Australian mainland was linked by land-bridges to Tasmania and New Guinea. Some 25,000–16,000 years ago the interior of Australia was subject to massive dust storms and sand dunes extended north to the Gulf of Carpentaria and southwards into eastern Victoria and Tasmania. Such events would have had marked impacts on the flora and fauna of Australia. However, that most recent period of severe aridity was only the last of many cycles of aridity associated with a long series of glacial–interglacial cycles in the Pleistocene.

Jim Bowler of the Australian National University has been much involved in unravelling this story. He indicates that about 2.5 million years ago global climates changed dramatically to give this long series of cold (glacial) and warmer (interglacial) periods. The cycles seem to have a regular frequency of about 100,000 years and some 19 cycles appear to have occurred. Since the megafauna had survived numerous severe arid cycles it is very unlikely that they would all succumb to the most recent one. Aboriginal people were the only significant new feature in the Australian megafaunal scene in the late Pleistocene. Besides, most of the megafauna groups became extinct before the significant impact of the last period of aridity which occurred between 20,000 and 17,000 years ago.

The role of fire in this story is still not well understood. Records from sediment cores taken from old lake beds show that fire has long been a factor in the Australian landscape. Lightning is still a prime cause of natural wildfires and the many plants that are either fire-resistant (such as eucalyptus trees) or require fire to complete their life cycles existed long before the arrival of Aborigines. That the arrival of Aborigines increased the frequency and changed the pattern of fires is accepted. Aborigines used fire to 'clean up' their country so that they could move around it more easily and also concentrate game on areas of new green pick; they still do so in northern Australia. They also use it to hunt. I have seen a marvellous early film of central Australian people using fire to flush out rat-kangaroos in their hunts.

The fire regime was, consequently, changed by Aborigines to one of more frequent but less intense fire. The net effect would have been less scrub and more open country with more ground plants, particularly grasses. Such conditions should have favoured large herbivores, the basis of the megafauna.

Direct evidence of Aborigines hunting and butchering megafauna is now becoming available. An excellent site at Cuddie Springs in north-western New South Wales has recently been reported on by Judith Furby and Bob Jones from the University of New South Wales and the Australian Museum. At this site analysis of plant pollens and soil profiles has revealed a paleo-environmental record spanning the late Pleistocene, including the period when the megafauna disappeared. The vegetation history at Cuddie Springs covers a time sequence not previously recorded in arid and semi-arid country. Aboriginal stone artefacts occur in direct association with the bones of diprotodons and sthenurine kangaroos at a level dated to 30,000 years ago. This find is exceptional because sites where large mammals were killed and butchered (and the bones eaten and scattered by scavengers) would not generally be expected to represent ideal conditions for fossilisation.

The impact of hunting can be demonstrated dramatically by the pattern of extinctions among the kangaroos. The large group of sthenurine 'kanga-roos' were totally removed from the Australian scene, even species that were smaller than living kangaroos; yet the macropodines, on the whole, suffered fewer extinctions, with survivors undergoing only a size reduction. The eastern grey kangaroo is probably a 'dwarfed' form of its predecessor *Macropus titan*. Why was there this differential survival among the different types of 'kangaroo'?

Peter Murray examined the functional anatomy of skeletons of both groups, particularly the pelvis and hind legs, and demonstrated that there were fundamental locomotor and postural differences between the sthenurines and the macropodines. The sthenurines were thickset kanga-roos with shorter and thicker hind limbs than those of the slender macro-podines. The principal differences lay in the functional mechanism of the hip and thigh. Generally, the sthenurines had longer and stouter femurs (upper leg bones) and the muscle attachments were such that they had a more powerful and faster retracting mechanism at the hip than the macro-podines had. However, the tibia (the main lower leg bone) was relatively shorter, resulting in a 'lower geared' hopping system. The sthenurines apparently went in for short bursts of rapid bounding and their predator avoidance strategy was a short sprint for cover. Although they would have had a quick take-off, they would not have been nearly as fast as the macro-podines at full speed; nor would they have been able to maintain speed for as long. Humans were persistent and organised hunters and it appears that the large stout sthenurine kangaroos were much more often their dinner than were the more slender, and faster, macropodine kangaroos that we see today. It seems that eventually a balance was reached and the red and grey kangaroos survived, the last of our megafauna.

# THE CURRENT SIGNIFICANCE OF KANGAROOS TO ABORIGINES

Before their way of life was so drastically altered by the impact of Europeans, Aborigines used kangaroos for a wide variety of purposes. Indeed, kangaroos are deeply embedded in the art and mythology of Aboriginal Australians. Nevertheless, in the relationship between Aborigines and kangaroos the matter of food was the primary focus. Among people living away from the coast kangaroos were often a mainstay of their diet. This can be seen from recently collected information on the diets of the Gunwingu people at outstations in Arnhem Land in the far north of Australia. These people consume a wide range of animals, almost 100 species of vertebrates and invertebrates, and a similar number of plants. But mammals were found to provide 84 per cent of the energy intake in the wet season and 91 per cent in the late dry season. Seven of the 14 species of mammals eaten were kangaroos or wallabies and these provided more than half of the energy intake.

Kangaroos and wallabies were hunted by methods which varied from district to district. In some areas kangaroos were mostly stalked quietly and speared. At times, groups of hunters combined; one group drove the kangaroos toward another group lying in ambush, and the kangaroos were killed with a spear or waddy. In particularly hilly country with distinct animal tracks large pitfall traps tended to be the most common method of catching kangaroos. Often seasonal conditions changed the method of hunting, because, in dry times kangaroos concentrated near water and in wet seasons they dispersed over the landscape.

From various parts of Australia there are descriptions of the traditional lifestyles of Aboriginal people and their intricate involvement with all aspects of their environment. Over the years, as I moved about Fowlers Gap Research Station in the Barrier Ranges of far western New South Wales, I wondered how the original people of the area had used and lived off the land. Signs of their past presence occur throughout the ranges and adjoining plains. Stone tools and the chips resulting from their manufacture are frequently found and easily identified, since the tools are made from a pale yellow stone which does not occur naturally on or near Fowlers Gap Station. Broken grinding stones and the smooth stones of old cooking fires also dot the flats along the creeks.

Some insight into the way of life of the Aboriginal inhabitants of this part of Australia and into their interaction with native mammals has been gained recently through Dorothy Tunbridge's studies involving Aboriginal people in the nearby Flinders Ranges of South Australia. The Flinders Ranges are just on the opposite side of the Lake Frome basin from the Barrier Ranges. I have been told that the people, animals and environment were very similar throughout these ranges before Europeans heedlessly devastated the land and its people.

# THE ADNYAMATHANHA PEOPLE OF THE FLINDERS RANGES — A CASE STUDY

Dorothy Tunbridge is a linguist-ethnographer who works with the Aboriginal people of the Flinders Ranges, specifically the Adnyamathanha people of the northern Flinders Ranges. Out of a discovery that there were Adnyamathanha words for animals that no living person had seen, a project developed that documented the destruction of an entire ecosystem and the way of life of a people who were an integral part of it. Tunbridge's study focused on the mammals and showed that of 45 terrestrial species 30 became extinct in the Flinders Ranges within the first 50 years of European settlement, or very shortly after. In her collaborative research with the Adnyamathanha people much information came to light on the vital role of kangaroos and wallabies in the people's traditional way of life. The red kangaroo is now the only native mammal that is hunted by these people — now with a rifle, sometimes with the aid of dogs. This traditional meat is still highly regarded and keenly sought.

Virtually all mammals were potential food for the traditional Adnyamathanha. Meat was the major part of their diet. Kangaroos, mainly red kangaroos and euros, were a natural favourite because they could feed a considerable number of people. As well, they were plentiful and easy to locate and hunting them was a well-developed art. The small mammals were generally eaten when the kangaroos and wallabies were not available, as in wet weather, when these big animals did not need to come to their traditional watering places.

## HUNTING KANGAROOS

Dorothy Tunbridge used many sources, including the recollections of living elders and records from the 19th century, to gain details of hunting patterns of the Adnyamathanha. I can but briefly summarise her reports. I strongly recommend that her account be read in detail: the story is told in the terms and language of the Adnyamathanha and it has life. Attendant with hunting was much ritual. Many dreamtime stories refer to hunting and to kangaroos.

The hunting of large game was the province of men, while women were mainly occupied with gathering plant food and small game. However, at

**Figure 9.3**
*The favoured
hunting weapons of
the Adnyamathanha
people of the
Flinders Ranges of
South Australia:
(A) waddy (wirri);
(B) boomerang
(wadna); (C) small
throwing spear
(aya). Fighting
forms of these
weapons were
distinct, principally
in being bigger and
heavier, such as (D)
the fighting spear
(wardlatha). After
Tunbridge (1991).*

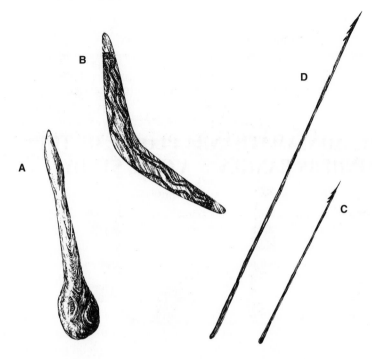

times women and even small children joined in a hunt for large game
when it was desirable to have the numbers to block off escape routes.
Surprisingly, the Adnyamathanha did not use the spear much for hunting
and when they did they favoured a short spear only about a metre long.
Their bigger spear, over twice as long, was a fighting spear. The small
spear was thrown either from the shoulder or underhand from the hip and
could travel faster than the big spear. A spearthrower was not used. In the
ranges where the Adnyamathanha generally lived, the narrow gorges, permanent waterholes and restricted tracks favoured trapping and close-up
missile throwing.

The favoured hunting implement was a large waddy and the second
preference was a non-returning hunting boomerang (Fig. 9.3). Both were
about half a metre long and were solid, being made of mulga wood. The
waddy had a bulge on one end and, as with the boomerang, was either
thrown or used as a club. A moving kangaroo could be brought down at up
to 50 metres if hit in the head or upper body. Occasionally kangaroos would
be chased to exhaustion, sometimes with dogs/dingos, but generally hides
near water or next to kangaroo pads were used to get within killing range.

Alternatively, the kangaroos could be driven to ambush in either natural
traps or constructed wing traps made of sticks and brush, with stones to
keep the brush in place. Instead of men waiting in ambush at the end of the
trap there could be a deep covered pit. Such pits were large, about 2.5 m

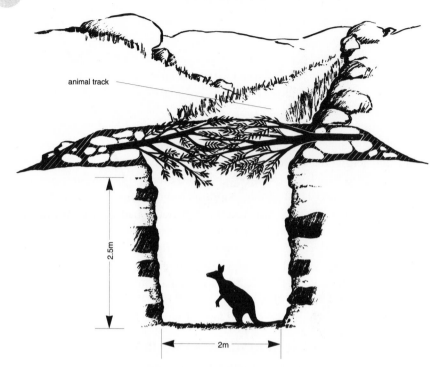

animal track

2.5m

2m

**Figure 9.4**
*A large pitfall trap
(vata) used by the
Adnyamathanha
people to catch
rock-wallabies and
kangaroos. It was
particularly
effective, being dug
on an animal pad
and camouflaged
with greenery
attractive to the
animals. After
Tunbridge (1991).*

deep and 2 m wide, so that kangaroos and wallabies could not escape. These traps were also placed in kangaroo pads and covered with a green vegetation that was attractive to kangaroos. The greenery was anchored at the edges so that it would spring back and remain in place once the animals had fallen in (Fig. 9.4). In this way more than one animal could be caught. The pits were regularly checked and any game in them killed before removal. There are still remnants of such traps in the Flinders Ranges.

Special nets were sometimes used at the end of the wing traps. One such net was about a metre high and 3–6 m wide. It was attached to trees or stakes and had drawstrings that closed the net when an animal rushed into it. The animal was thus entangled and held until it could be killed with a waddy. This type of net was usually used for smaller game such as rock-wallabies. A larger net designed for catching red kangaroos, euros and emus was used in a different way. Its mesh was bigger and it was used near watering places. This net was about 1.75 m high and 80–90 m long and was very light and compact for its size. It was made of strong twine formed from either wallaby tail sinews or string from plant fibres. It was attached at one end to a tree, then laid flat and camouflaged on the ground across, say, a kangaroo pad that led to water. While an animal was drinking it was deliberately disturbed by a hunter. As it set off back the way it had come, the net would be raised and it would be entangled and clubbed. This sounds well organised but, as I know from catching them with cannon nets at sheep water troughs on Fowlers Gap Station (Plate 11), kangaroos are quite adept at struggling out of nets. I can well imagine the hunters' mad rush to get to their kangaroo before it managed to free itself. We have often snared kangaroos in this manner, but when we rushed in to claim our catch we carried syringes of tranquilliser and large holding sacks instead of waddies and boomerangs.

I used to wonder how dead kangaroos were carried back to camp, especially by a single hunter. I have often stalked euros in the hills of Fowlers Gap, and getting the quarry back to the truck for processing is a significant problem. Lugging a kangaroo is very awkward even if it is only for a couple of hundred metres. The technique appears to be to carry it on your head. (H. H. Finlayson of the South Australian Museum had a photo of this in his fascinating book *The Red Centre*, which describes his travels in central Australia during 1931–35.) The kangaroo was first gutted and its legs dislocated at the first joint. The head was then forced down between the legs to the base of the tail, so that the trunk was flexed in a circle. The forelegs and tail were then tied with a length of gut. The resulting circular bundle was hoisted on the head and carried long distances.

## COOKING AND BUTCHERING OF KANGAROOS

The red kangaroo was clearly favoured by Aborigines as the best species to eat. Euro meat is darker and the fat more yellow; the euro was said to be less tasty than the red kangaroo. The western grey kangaroo was not liked by the Adnyamathanha because it smelled too much. In fact, only the males smell; Dorothy Tunbridge suggests that a tradition of eating western grey kangaroo had not developed because it moved into Adnyamathanha country only in the past 20–30 years.

The main method of cooking a kangaroo was to roast it in a ground oven; basically, cooking it in the ashes. A hole was dug in the ground a little bigger than the kangaroo and a good fire made in it. The fire was allowed to burn down and the kangaroo placed on the coals. If the animal had been skinned fresh leaves were first placed on the coals. The kangaroo was then covered with leaves, coals and hot ash; earth was used as a final cover. Sometimes small smooth creek stones were used in place of, or as well as, the leaves. Heated stones were often placed in the gut cavity of big animals to give more even cooking. Piles of stones from the ground ovens appear on creek flats throughout the Barrier Ranges.

How much cooking was given to a kangaroo is debated. Finlayson reported that the central Australian people left it in a ground oven for only about half an hour and that the bulk of the meat was quite raw, often scarcely hot. He wondered why the people did not dispense with 'the fire process altogether'. The Adnyamathanha presumably took their meat 'rare'. I have been told by Aboriginal people in western New South Wales that

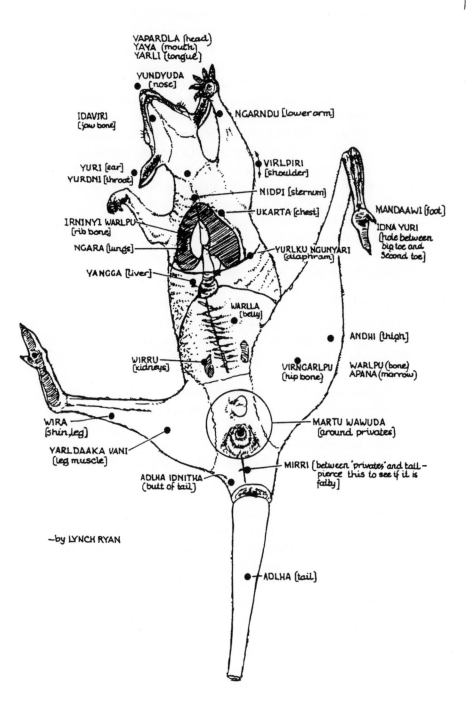

**Figure 9.5**
*The parts of a red kangaroo with their Adnyamathanha names as they relate to food and butchering. A drawing by the late Lynch Ryan, an Adnyamathanha elder. Reprinted, with permission, from Tunbridge (1991).*

two to three hours is needed for cooking a kangaroo. In my experience that would be a bare minimum!

When a kangaroo was cooked a large creek stone was selected as a chopping block, and the animal was chopped and cut up with a stone chopper made from a hand-sized creek stone. If available, stone-ground axes were preferred; these were obtained by trading with people further north. The meat was cut up and distributed only by an older initiated man (see Fig. 9.5 for parts of a red kangaroo and their names). Virtually all parts of the kangaroo were eaten, but not everyone was permitted to eat all parts. There were strict food taboos and basically the best cuts were reserved for the elders, the older initiated men and old women. Of note, these were the only people allowed to eat female euros. The elders could eat any part of a kangaroo and were the only ones who could eat the hip bone, all the tail and the head. The various age and sex groups had different taboos.

For young women and unmarried girls the 'big thing' was the tail. They were absolutely forbidden the upper tail and tail butt. Girls who broke this law would be punished by having considerable trouble in pregnancy. The baby, it was said, would become entangled in the sinews. They were permitted to eat the lower leg and arms and also the back of the neck, but not the head. Young boys were even more restricted, being limited to the ribs, the lower leg and a couple of tail joints. There were all sorts of problems in store for them if they broke these laws. Eating the hip bone or forbidden parts of the tail could affect their virility; they could discover that they were impotent when they married.

There is a perception that traditional Aboriginal people did not store or process meat; this is not true. The Adnyamathanha dried and stored meat as well as fruit. The meat was called *vityurna* and was made from red kangaroo, euro and rock-wallaby meat. An animal was cooked in the ashes with its skin on. It was taken out and placed on fresh green boughs and then the skin was peeled off. The meat was cut into 3–10 cm strips and air-dried (being covered to keep the flies away). Salt was not used until the coming of Europeans. The *vityurna* was stored in a skin bag and used in times of food shortage. It was eaten dry after being pounded with creek stones. A sausage was also made using the foregut of a red kangaroo as the casing. The liver and kidneys were chopped up and placed in the casing with kidney fat; blood was then poured in and the casing sealed. It was cooked in the ashes. Apparently a good sausage had plenty of blood.

## KANGAROO PRODUCTS

Skin products were the most obvious of the items manufactured from kangaroos. Skins were used to make a blanket or rug, which was used also as a cloak, a bone pin holding it at the front. The blanket was in fact a general utility item. For instance, it could be used to catch insects or fruit when they were shaken out of trees. Water bags and general carrying bags were also made out of kangaroo skins; however, the Adnyamathanha favoured the yellow-footed rock-wallaby for water bags and possum skins for carry bags. The skins were tanned after they had been pegged out to dry for a day or two. Tanning was carried out by soaking a skin in water with lots of leaves of the native plum or emubush, *Eremophila longifolia*. This took two to four days, after which the skin was dried and the inner surface scraped to remove meat and fat and to make the skin softer.

If a water bag was to be made the kangaroo was skinned with great care. The animal was cut around the neck and the skin of the arms and shoulder loosened. The arms were cut above the forepaws and pulled out, and the skin worked down over the body. The tail was cut off, the butt skin being used as a closing flap. The hind leg skins were split and tied together to form a carrying strap. The bottom of the bag was sealed by binding the arms and neck with strong sinew twine.

Sinew twine made from the tail sinews had many utilitarian uses. Apart from tying up bags it was used for sewing skin blankets and making nets, especially the big nets used for catching red kangaroos and euros. The sinews were removed from the tail by winding them on to a stick. They were then stretched and dried; after which they were greased with fat, rolled into a ball and kept dry. To make twine for a net two sinews of uneven length were rolled together on the thigh so that they twisted together. Another piece of sinew was added at the end of each twisted sinew until the rope became as long as required. For nets the sinew twine was preferred over twine made from hair or fur because it was much stronger. Hair twine was made from human hair or animal fur. Possum fur was preferred. Euro fur was also used, but red kangaroo fur was little used because the fibres were too short. The twine or string was made by teasing the fur or hair into a ball and then spinning it on to a spindle. The spindle was made of a wooden shaft with crosspieces. The spinning was done by twisting the spindle on the thigh.

The Adnyamathanha of the northern Flinders Ranges were dependent on the mammals of the area for their survival. Not only were they a vital source of food but they were also used in the manufacturing of products that were important in the economy and the rich daily life of the people. The coming of European settlement simply destroyed the people's environment and eliminated many of their animals. True, the kangaroos survived but even they were decimated at first. The overall change has been too great for another satisfactory environmental balance to be easily achieved. Australia is now searching for a new and appropriate balance between its peoples and its land. The completeness of the land and its Aboriginal people, with their rich traditions and insights, is just too precious for us to allow old destructive patterns to continue.

# KANGAROOS AND HUMAN — EUROPEANS

## FIRST ENCOUNTERS

We often accept that it was the voyagers on the *Endeavour* with Captain Cook who produced the first European records of kangaroos and their exceptional forms of locomotion and reproduction. While this may be true for the large kangaroos, it is not the case for the macropodines in general. Perhaps the first recorded description of a kangaroo or wallaby was made by the Dutch seaman merchant Francisco Pelsaert. In 1629, while rescuing survivors of the *Batavia*, which had been wrecked off the coast of what is now Western Australia near the present town of Geraldton, Pelsaert described what was probably the tammar wallaby, *Macropus eugenii*. That these animals had a pouch and were marsupials like the opossums of the Americas was soon accepted, but the mode of giving birth was confusing. After describing the wallaby, and noting the structure of the pouch, Pelsaert suggested that the young grew directly out of the nipples. This myth persisted for hundreds of years despite evidence to the contrary.

Numerous sighting of macropodines were made by the Dutch in the course of the next hundred years as they explored, often accidentally, the western coast of New Holland (as Australia had come to be known after

1642) in connection with their trading interests in the East Indies. The reports arising from these activities had little impact on the scientific community in Europe. Things began to change with the voyages of the Englishman William Dampier. Dampier was a member of a privateering expedition on the *Cygnet* which visited New Holland in 1688. This visit was part of a circumnavigation of the world, and Dampier's edited journal *A New Voyage Round the World*, published in 1697, brought him to the notice of the naval and scientific community in England.

The English were interested in New Holland and the rich East Indies of the Dutch; oddly, the Dutch did not provide much information for their competitors. Dampier was subsequently offered the command of the *Roebuck* by the Admiralty for a voyage to New Holland. While the voyage was beset with problems — the *Roebuck* in fact foundered toward the end — Dampier had an insatiable curiosity and kept an accurate and detailed account of the scientific aspects of the voyage. In *A voyage to New Holland* he recounts his adventures and discoveries of 1699–1700. Among his descriptions of the fauna of New Holland is one of '... a Sort of Racoons, different from those of the West Indies; chiefly as to their Legs; for these have very short Fore-legs; but go jumping upon them as the others do ...' The identity of this macropodid is uncertain but the wide acceptance of Dampier's work meant that when kangaroos were found and collected by the scientists on the *Endeavour* in 1770 they were not as novel as is generally believed.

In the latter part of the 1700s interest in science and far lands blossomed and expeditions from several nations were despatched to our corner of the world. The stories of their discoveries, as well as their numerous trials and tribulations, are remarkable. There are many accounts of these events but I particularly enjoy one given by Colin Finney. His book *To Sail Beyond the Sunset: Natural History in Australia 1699–1829* also recounts the early years of the colony of New South Wales, including the first expeditions into the interior. These years brought the unfolding of knowledge of our unique flora and fauna; the adventures in natural history make fascinating reading.

## ATTITUDES TO KANGAROOS, THEN AND NOW

In the early days of Australia there was intense curiosity about the nature of kangaroos, and this persists. I have had overseas colleagues accompany me to Fowlers Gap Research Station and once among the red kangaroos moving gracefully over the open plains they are overwhelmed. The same applies to many Australian city dwellers (i.e. most Australians). The significance of all this to our feeling for the nature of our country, and to tourism, is still greatly underestimated. While there are now national parks in the interior with good populations of kangaroos, there are still very few places within a short distance of our major cities where numbers of kangaroos can be seen in their natural condition. The Royal National Park just south of Sydney until very recently protected imported European deer as an attraction, much to the detriment of a reasonable population of eastern grey kangaroos!

That fertile land is required for the plant production needed to maintain good numbers of herbivores, be they kangaroos or koalas, is still not well recognised. This, of course, is the land desired for farms, grazing runs and productive forests. We have not yet generally accepted the great benefit of giving up even a small portion of this land to our natural heritage. We will, however; and we will prove wrong that most famous of all 'ecotourists', Charles Darwin. When he visited Sydney in 1836 he hired a man and two horses to take him to the village of Bathurst, 120 miles into the interior. By this means Darwin hoped to gain a general idea of the country and its natural history. Over the mountains at a large farm called 'Walerawang' he was taken kangaroo hunting. The party had bad sport, not even seeing a kangaroo. Darwin commented: 'A few years since this country abounded with wild animals; but now the emu is banished to a long distance, and the kangaroo is become scarce; to both the English greyhound has been highly destructive. It may be long before these animals are altogether exterminated, but their doom is fixed.'

Apart from curiosity about the species the early colonists had a fourfold interest in kangaroos: meat, skins, sport, or vermin competing with their flocks of sheep. Little has changed in the past two centuries, except that the level of importance placed on each of these interests has varied with time. It continues to vary, as indicated by the recent change in public attitude to the human consumption of kangaroo meat.

## KANGAROOS AS MEAT

One of the earliest interests in kangaroos was whether they were edible and, if so, what was the quality of the meat. This attitude was natural for the first explorers on our coasts because meat in ships' rations was heavily salted. Fresh meat other than fish was very welcome and in the quantities provided by a kangaroo it was a luxury. On 14 July 1770 the first kangaroo (as distinct from a wallaby) was obtained by Cook's party at Endeavour River. It was shot by Lieutenant John Gore. Cook that day recorded the details of the animal and its mode of progression. The next day the entry in Cook's journal records: 'Today we din'd of the animal shott yesterday & thought it excellent food'.

Not everyone thought highly of kangaroo meat. Governor Phillip thought its flesh 'coarse and lean' and considered that it probably would not be used but for the scarcity of fresh provisions. Still, it was included on the menu of His Majesty's Birthday Dinner which Phillip presided over on 4 June

1788. Kangaroos (eastern grey kangaroos) soon became equated with meat in the colony of New South Wales. The Governor employed a shooter and convicts were assigned to hunt kangaroos for public consumption.

Two centuries later this early attitude that kangaroo (and emu) were food was extensively documented by Martin Denny in a report to the Australian National Parks and Wildlife Service. He was trying to establish the densities of kangaroos in the early days, relative to current numbers. Many extracts from the journals of explorers and early travellers indicate that kangaroo and emu were regarded simply as food and not a curiosity worth mentioning in their travels. The same attitude persisted in rural areas for almost a hundred years.

In Steele Rudd's classic 'Our Selection' stories, based on the lives of set-tlers in the Darling Downs of Queensland about a hundred years ago, the meat was kangaroo. But in these stories we also see the reason why kangaroo dropped *off* our menus: social pressure. The story of Kate's wedding illus-trated this well: Dad was most embarrassed by the kangaroo leg hanging on the veranda when the parson came; he tried to pass it off as being for the dog.

The dog was a 'kangaroo dog', a breed that was used in hunting kanga-roos. These crossbred greyhounds were still used for kangaroo hunting when I was growing up in the small inland New South Wales town of Nyngan. I still remember the tales of the exploits of a kangaroo dog belong-ing to our neighbours. By then, though, the hunts provided sport and the meat *was* for the dogs.

The pattern of life revealed in the 'Our Selection' stories reflects the stories my grandmother told, when in later life she realised that my family was inter-ested in the 'early years'. She remained sharp-minded into her nineties and readily told of life on settlers' runs on the Macquarie and Castlereagh Rivers of New South Wales. Kangaroos and wallabies, and especially emus and their eggs, were common fare 'early on', but as prosperity improved they were dropped from the diet. The reason: to eat kangaroo was to indicate that you couldn't afford to kill your own sheep and that you were poor.

The stigma on kangaroo meat, having developed for social reasons, con-tinued long after the reason was perhaps forgotten. And kangaroo is still rarely eaten on the pastoral stations on the plains — the reason given is 'worms'. In fact, it became illegal to sell kangaroo meat for human con-sumption under a 'Health Act' in New South Wales. 'Worms' are also the reason given for not eating emu, feral pig, feral goat and (sometimes) rabbit. Yet, generally, these animals carry many fewer diseases and parasites than do the sheep or cattle that provide such a monotonous diet in grazing country.

Throughout Australia kangaroo is once again on the table, now legally, though as yet mainly in fashionable restaurants: except, that is, for the tables of those Aboriginal people who never gave up their preference for it. Why the change? I think it is a natural outcome of the intense debate about kangaroos over the last three decades. At the beginning of this debate there were extreme attitudes and little factual information. As all aspects of kangaroos were examined in detail it was reasonable that the social prohibition on eating them should be questioned, once it was seen that kangaroos were not threatened species. This was particularly so when other game meat, such as venison and buffalo, started to become fashionable.

One has to bear in mind that while this argument was going on the Australia-wide annual quota for kangaroos for pet food and skins approached three million. A good account of most aspects of the commercial kangaroo industry (in Queensland) is provided in *The Kangaroo Keepers*, edited by Hugh Lavery in 1985.

The basic premise put forward by those who advocated human consumption of kangaroo meat was that it would result in more effective use of kangaroos. Kangaroos would be valued more highly and they would be conserved and managed as a renewable resource. If graziers were able to get some value out of kangaroos they might be able to reduce the grazing pressure from hard-footed domestic stock and better manage our fragile semi-arid and arid lands.

An excellent symposium on this topic in 1988 had all viewpoints represented. Its report was entitled *Kangaroo Harvesting and the Conservation of Arid and Semi-arid Lands*; edited by Dan Lunney and Gordon Grigg. I recommend it to anyone interested in this controversial topic. The myths about eating kangaroo were banished. Rather than being a health problem kangaroo meat presents fewer problems than does domestic stock, provided that the proper guidelines are followed. Current state legislation is similar to the Commonwealth legislation for export quality kangaroo for human consumption which was outlined by A. E. Andrews, of the Australian Quarantine and Inspection Service.

Basically, the legislation requires that:

- the animal must be shot in the head, not only to ensure a quick kill but also to prevent damage to the skin, carcase and internal organs which are required for health inspection purposes

- the kangaroo must be bled and gutted immediately, with the liver, spleen and kidneys remaining attached to the carcase

- the carcase must be placed under refrigeration within two hours of being shot or, where the animal is shot at night, not more than two hours after sunrise

- deep muscle temperature must be reduced to below 7°C within 12 hours and maintained until inspection

- standards of inspection by qualified meat inspectors and of the processing facilities must be the same as those for domestic animals.

Because the methods of shooting and handling in the field may be conducive to contamination and spoilage, emphasis is placed on hygienic handling at every stage. Inspection records for animals processed show that kangaroos treated in this manner compare most favourably with normally slaughtered domestic animals.

In other health respects kangaroo meat has advantages. It is low in fat, a high proportion of which is polyunsaturated. Kerin O'Dea of the Department of Human Nutrition at Deakin University carried out dietary studies with Australians of European origin and Aborigines. She showed that low-fat diets rich in kangaroo meat were associated with a reduction in important risk factors for cardiovascular diseases.

For cooking and serving there are many good old recipes for kangaroo. The meat may be treated in the manner of venison with good results. Elizabeth May, who cooked for several of my student field camps, adapted beef bourguignon to great effect. The flavour of kangaroo meat also comes through nicely in a good curry. However, if kangaroo meat is to be treated as 'steak', that is grilled or fried, then it should, like all game, be hung for several days if taken in the field. Only once have I tried to eat kangaroo acquired on the same day. It was almost as tough as a rabbit that Martin Denny shot an hour or so before we tried to eat it when we ran out of food while surveying euros one year in the Flinders Ranges.

As to how the making of kangaroo readily available for human consumption will impact on kangaroo numbers and the species' conservation, I am unsure. I suspect that kangaroo will be only a speciality meat for the foreseeable future. This would mean that the quota numbers diverted for the table market would have little impact on current populations. That the human consumption of kangaroo meat will lead to wider acceptance that kangaroos have value and are not just vermin is likely. How this will transpose into a greater interest in conservation on the part of the general public and into a more tolerant and positive attitude on the part of landholders only time will tell. On the other side of the coin, it has been suggested that an increase in the acceptance of kangaroo for human consumption will lead to more illegal hunting. This may be true, but many kangaroos are already hunted illegally for sport — the justification being that they are 'vermin'. Perhaps if kangaroos are more highly valued this behaviour will diminish.

## THE USE OF KANGAROO SKINS FOR LEATHER

While there has been much focus on the harvesting of kangaroos for meat, either as pet food or for human consumption, the skin trade has been the traditional base for commercial exploitation. The kangaroo skin trade was developed on a large scale in the middle of the 19th century. For many years the kangaroo shooter with his trained 'shooting' horse and packhorses was a part of the character of country districts. Kangaroo leather is a light, good quality leather and was used for the uppers of shoes and boots (shoes, especially running and sport shoes, still feature among its uses). Martin Denny established that a steady half million skins a year passed through the Melbourne market alone in the last half of the 19th century — and this was but one of the large markets. The skin market was developed largely to service European and American processors, particularly the latter. A specialised industry grew up on the east coast of the United States. Through a joint buying scheme these tanners effectively controlled the trade in skins until the meat market (pet food) developed in the 1950s and 1960s. The skin trade was completely disrupted by the conservation-inspired closure of the United States market from 1973 to 1981. The commercial exploitation of kangaroos for skins is now established again.

The economics of the trade is that it is still often more profitable to shoot kangaroos only for their skins. While the total return per animal is much less than if the carcase is also used for meat, the overheads are lower. There are problems with skin-only shooting because of the greater focus on large animals as well as the perceived waste of resources (i.e. the meat). Skin-only shooting is consequently restricted in New South Wales but not in Queensland where most kangaroos are harvested. In the mid-1980s skin-only shooting comprised 60 per cent of the commercial kill.

## KANGAROO FARMING?

If kangaroos are a valuable resource why not farm them instead of killing the wild population? Deer are farmed — for venison, leather and antlers. The current exploitation of kangaroos is seen as a population management measure. The present management system has mixed objectives: conservation of wild kangaroos and alleviation of damage to agriculture. Commercial decisions are supposedly secondary to these aims. Kangaroo farming, on the other hand, would be solely directed at getting a sustained income from the enterprise. It is likely that current management plans and farming would conflict.

Neil Shepherd, then of the New South Wales National Parks and Wildlife Service, reviewed the feasibility of farming kangaroos. He considered a range of aspects from marketing to legal and administrative difficulties. Two possible systems were examined: intensive farming and rangeland farming.

Production under intensive conditions (as used in the deer industry) would be restricted by low reproduction and slow growth rates. There would also be handling and husbandry difficulties. Rangeland farming (as distinct from managed rangeland culling) would have difficulties due to the mobility of kangaroos, the amount and type of fencing needed and kangaroo behaviour that makes mustering unworkable. These problems could perhaps be overcome if the economics was on the side of farming.

However, any farming enterprise would have to compete with the existing managed conservation cull. This cull generally does not reach its quotas, largely for cost reasons. Consequently, it appears that kangaroo farming is simply not economically feasible at this stage. Refinement of the current system to allow for greater involvement of landholders in its management and its economic returns could be beneficial.

## KANGAROOS AS SPORT

The idea of using kangaroos for sport is one that is now poorly regarded by many Australians, but this was not always so. Apart from the hunting of kangaroos for meat, which often had sport as a twin purpose, kangaroos were often hunted in the manner of the English foxhunt (Fig. 10.1). This was especially the case early in the 19th century when kangaroos were relatively common near settled areas. Settlers who were familiar with coursing for fox or hare in England simply substituted the kangaroo. The sport became very popular and clubs were established using the same rules as did those in England. Interestingly enough one club, the Cumberland Hounds, was sited near Homebush, now a suburb of Sydney at which the Olympic Games will be held in 2000.

Many descriptions of hunts exist. Most are told in a heroic vein and recount dashes on marvellous horses through broken scrub. In John

*Figure 10.1*
*In the 19th century kangaroo hunting by 'riding the hounds' was considered great sport. The hounds were special 'kangaroo dogs', derived largely from the English greyhound. Detail of the painting* A kangaroo hunt under Mount Zero *by Edward Roper.*

Gould's 1863 volume on kangaroos an account is given of a hunt in which a 'boomer' was pursued for over two hours, in which time it covered at least 30 km. The boomer in question was a large eastern grey buck and the hunt was conducted in Tasmania. The species almost became extinct in that island state. While hunts were frequently pictured as heroic and dashing, in reality they were probably often more like the activity described by Steele Rudd in 'A kangaroo hunt from shingle hut' in *On Our Selection*. This form of hunting seems long gone but I can attest that a rough form of it persisted until the 1950s at least. The dogs in this case were carried on the back of a 'ute' or open truck. The aim was to get close enough to the kangaroo so that the vehicle could be rapidly stopped and the dogs let off to bail up the animal. The kangaroo was then dispatched with a waddy. If the driver misjudged the stop and the kangaroo got moving well it generally escaped. In more open country the kangaroo would be chased in the truck to cut it off from the scrub before the dogs were let off.

Hunting kangaroos via individual stalking has not become the sport that large game hunting (e.g. for deer) has in other parts of the world. The deer season in the United States is notable for the number of people taking part and its economic consequences. Deer licences are expensive and often cover only one or two animals. Whole conservation programs are based on the resulting revenue. Such hunting is now illegal in Australia and I cannot see it being re-established here, at least in the foreseeable future.

## KANGAROOS AS AGRICULTURAL 'PESTS'

Early settlers soon learned that kangaroos and wallabies were herbivores, apparently using the same feed as did their imported domestic animals. They also ate valuable young crops. To their sorrow, the settlers found that much of the country was not as fertile nor was it as regularly watered as the farmlands of Europe. So, when the long-accumulated reserves of vegetation were eaten away and the inevitable drought came, disaster struck. Again I refer you to Dorothy Tunbridge's story of the Flinders Ranges.

Not being totally able to blame themselves, in their ignorance and greed, the settlers focused on the 'vermin' kangaroos as one of their main problems — kangaroos being big and obvious. As early as the 1860s sheep farmers were complaining and calling for action against kangaroo 'plagues'. It is not known if there was a marked increase in numbers or whether the kangaroo numbers had previously been high. If there was an increase the reasons may have included a reduction of predators (i.e. dingos and Aborigines), increased available forage due to tree clearing and shrub reduction, and the provision of more watering points.

Martin Denny in his examination of early records noted the change from hunting for sport to hunting for pest eradication. All eastern states enacted legislation encouraging the destruction of kangaroos and other noxious animals. The NSW *Pastures and Stock Protection Act* of 1882 stated: 'Whereas the depredation of rabbits, native dogs and marsupials in many districts of this colony have inflicted serious damage and loss on stock-owners it is necessary … to encourage the destruction of such animals'. By 1902 it had become 'the duty' of landholders to suppress and destroy all rabbits and noxious animals, kangaroos being included in the latter category.

Mass destruction became the order of the day, especially in dry times when landholders feared for their stock and crops. A principal mode of eradication developed during this period was the kangaroo drive or 'battue'. This procedure was derived from the Aboriginal hunting method of driving kangaroos into an enclosed place, natural or constructed, and then killing them from an ambush. Often a fenced trap was used to contain the kangaroos so that few escaped the killing by waddy or rifle. Hundreds were regularly killed in a day by such techniques. Kangaroo drives were still taking place in the New England tablelands when I was a student at the University of New England in the late 1950s.

Government bounties were placed on kangaroo scalps at an early stage and more than a million scalps were returned each year during the latter part of the 19th century. This number did not include the private arrangements for scalp bounties made by landholders. Such arrangements have continued until recent times. Stations in the northern Flinders Ranges of South Australia were still paying bounties for red kangaroos and euros when Martin Denny and I were there in 1969. Poisoning has also been used on kangaroos in pest eradication campaigns. Massive poisoning campaigns were carried out in the rangelands of Western Australia through the middle of the 20th century. Particular instances are the eradication programs focusing on the euro in the Pilbara region.

## ARE KANGAROOS PESTS, AND IF SO WHAT DAMAGE DO THEY DO?

We have seen how farmers and graziers have tried to eradicate, or at least control kangaroo numbers. Were they justified? What was the level of damage attributable to kangaroos? The full answers to these questions are still not available, but we are getting closer to understanding what is happening. From this point of view the increased concern of the conservation movement since the 1960s has been valuable. It has meant that governments have increased funding of research into kangaroo biology. The result has been a marked increase in our knowledge about these most extraordinary mammals, some of which has been described in this book.

That landholders do suffer some economic loss through the activities of kangaroos (and other macropodines) is true. There are well-documented cases of kangaroos damaging cereal crops. There is evidence of competition between kangaroos and sheep for feed. Fences are damaged and scarce stock water is drunk by kangaroos. Hugh Lavery and Tom Kirkpatrick summarise perceptions of the problem in Queensland in *The Kangaroo Keepers*, and such general perceptions also apply in other states.

An assessment of the economic effects of kangaroos and kangaroo culling on agricultural production throughout a range of agricultural environments was attempted by Lucinda Gibson and Mike Young of CSIRO. They produced a report for the Australian National Parks and Wildlife Service entitled *Kangaroos: Counting the Cost*. This report described and analysed the results of an extensive survey of landholders throughout the commercial shooting area of mainland Australia. The survey was designed to identify landholders' perceptions of the effects which kangaroos are having on agricultural production. It tried to gain insight into the perceived costs of kangaroo activity. The consequences of closing down the commercial kangaroo industry were also canvassed. In all, 906 farmers and graziers in five pastoral zones, two marginal cropping regions and three established cropping areas were surveyed.

Around 1983–84 the estimated cost of the perceived losses was $A113 million, this being 3 per cent of the gross agricultural production in the areas then under the national kangaroo management program. Estimates of perceived losses of agricultural production ranged from 0.27 per cent in the North-west Pastoral Zone of South Australia to 6.85 per cent in the Goondiwindi region of southern Queensland. The opportunity cost of fodder eaten by kangaroos accounted for 51 per cent of estimated total agricultural losses. This factor was highest in the marginal cropping region around Walgett (NSW) (71%) and in the Broken Hill Pastoral Region in the far west of New South Wales (65%). Losses in crop production were estimated to make up 27 per cent of total agricultural losses, the opportunity cost of water consumed accounted for 8 per cent and the cost of fence repairs represented 14 per cent.

That kangaroos cause losses of agricultural production is not to be disputed. The *actual* level of losses — i.e. a figure based on the results of scientific research — is unknown. Losses are largely perceived to be due to competition for forage. Overall, landholders perceived losses in carrying capacity that were about 60 per cent of the maximum possible if kangaroos and livestock were competing directly for feed. Our studies at Fowlers Gap Station showed that most of the time there was no competition at all. It was only during dry periods that competition became a factor (actually impacting on kangaroos more than on sheep); not until drought arrived would competition reach important levels.

Problems with provision of water and crop damage also seem to be exacerbated during dry times. The amount of water used by kangaroos is much overstated. In summer at Fowlers Gap the water turnover of kangaroos is only a quarter of that of sheep and much of this water they obtain from vegetation, even in dry times. Kangaroos actually drink much less than sheep do. In our work at Fowlers Gap, when sheep were watering twice a day, kangaroos were found to be watering about once a week on average; some watered as often as every third day. Our best estimate would be that a kangaroo drinks 10 per cent of the intake of a sheep. Still, there can be a lot of kangaroos and one sympathises with the drought-stricken grazier struggling to keep the water up to dry sheep. It is also during dry times that the impact on crops becomes significant. Even then, it is usually only young crops that are badly affected, especially those adjacent to timbered areas that provide the refuges for grey kangaroos.

The pattern of competition between sheep and kangaroo should vary with the type of country and the vegetation. What we see in the saltbush country of western New South Wales may not hold in other regions. To see whether this is the case more studies into possible levels of competition are needed. Unfortunately, these need to be long-term projects and they are difficult and expensive to carry out. Notwithstanding this, the perceived levels of production loss due to forage losses to kangaroos are likely to be overestimated. On the other hand, the number of kangaroos present over much of the grazing lands and marginal cropping zones is probably larger than perceived, particularly where there are significant timber and scrub refuges. This, together with the population dynamics of the various species of kangaroo, means that the financial benefit of killing more kangaroos is much less than is generally accepted. Graeme Caughley suggested, on the basis of computer simulation, that a continued commercial harvest of 10–15 per cent of the kangaroo population per year would reduce the population to 60–70 per cent of its unharvested density. If kangaroo densities are higher than previously considered such harvest levels would more than saturate any foreseeable market.

## THE CURRENT SITUATION — HAS A PROPER BALANCE BEEN REACHED?

What then is the current situation? Have we reached an adequate balance between the competing desires of different groups within the community? Basically, no, but we have come closer than we suspect except in the closer settled areas. We badly need some large national parks in our better farming country to give refuge to kangaroos (and probably more importantly to smaller wallabies, bettongs and bandicoots) and to make these animals accessible in their natural surroundings to urban Australians. The small Taunton Reserve near Dingo in central Queensland, which still contains the bridled nailtail wallaby and many other macropodines, provides an indication of what could be possible. In the rangelands we are probably closer to a balance than we think. There are acceptable numbers of kangaroos and the damage that they do to agricultural production is limited. The impact can, however, be severe in localised areas in dry times.

Can changes in our economic use of kangaroos help in the conservation of our degrading arid and semi-arid lands? Perhaps, but the basic responsibility is ours. I quote a statement made at the Kangaroo Harvesting symposium by Dean Graetz of CSIRO, a long-term conscience in regard to our ill-use of such lands.

> It must be recognised that, whatever the land use, whatever the herbivore harvested, conservative management of the land by man is still necessary. There are no 'natural' arid systems. Man will always have the responsibility because man, both black and white, has altered the land by his activities. How the land *will* be is a matter for management based on ecological understanding. How the land *should* be is meaningless.

We have a responsibility to 'get it right' in the management of our land and its kangaroos. This means that we have to decide what we consider is right. A reasonable consensus can be reached only if we have a true understanding of the ecosystems and their animal components. In the case of conservation of the six species of large kangaroo I hope that this book makes a positive contribution to such understanding.

# FURTHER READING

• • • • • • • • • • • • • • • • • • • • • • • • • • • • • • • • • • • • • • • • • • • • • • • • • • •

## CHAPTER 1

Archer, M., Hand, S. and Gohdhelp, H. (1991) *Riversleigh* Reed Publishers: Sydney

Dawson, T.J. and Taylor, C.R. (1973) Energetic cost of locomotion in kangaroos *Nature* 246: 313–14

Flannery, T. F. (1989) Phylogeny of the Macropodoidea: a study in convergence. In *Kangaroos, Wallabies and Rat-kangaroos* (eds Grigg, G., Jarman, P. and Hume, I.) Surrey Beatty & Sons: Chipping Norton, NSW

## CHAPTER 2

Caughley, G. (1987) Introduction to the sheep rangelands. In *Kangaroos: Their Ecology and Management in the Sheep Rangelands of Australia* (eds Caughley, G., Shepherd, N.C. and Short, J.) Cambridge University Press: Cambridge

Clancy, T.F. and Croft, D.B. (1992) Population dynamics of the common wallaroo (*Macropus robustus erubescens*) in arid New South Wales *Wildlife Research* 19: 1–16

Kirsh, J.A.W. and Poole, W.E. (1972) Taxonomy and distribution of the grey kangaroos, *Macropus giganteus* (Shaw) and *Macropus fuliginosus* (Desmarest), and their subspecies (Marsupialia: Macropodidae) *Australian J. Zoology* 20: 315–39

Press, A.J. (1988) The distribution and status of macropods in Kakadu National Park, Northern Territory, Australia *Australian Mammalogy* 11: 103–8

Richardson, B.J. and Sharman, G.B. (1976) Biochemical and morphological observations on the wallaroos (Macropodidae: Marsupialia) with a suggested new taxonomy *J. Zoology, London*, 176: 499–513

## CHAPTER 3

Arnold, G.W., Grassia, A., Steven, D.E. and Weeldenburg, J.R. (1991) Population ecology of western grey kangaroos in a remnant of wandoo woodland at Bakers Hill, southern Western Australia *Wildlife Research* 18: 561–75

Clancy, T.F. (1989) *Factors influencing movement patterns of the euro (Macropus robustus erubescens) in the Arid Zone* PhD thesis, University of New South Wales: Kensington

Clancy, T.F. and Croft, D.B. (1990) Home range of the common wallaroo, *Macropus robustus erubescens*, in far western New South Wales *Australian Wildlife Research* 17: 659–73

Clarke, J.L., Jones, M.E. and Jarman, P.J. (1989) A day in the life of a kangaroo: activities and movements of eastern grey kangaroos *Macropus giganteus* at Wallaby Creek. In *Kangaroos, Wallabies and Rat-kangaroos* (eds Grigg, G., Jarman, P. and Hume, I.) Surrey Beatty & Sons: Chipping Norton, NSW

Croft, D.B. (1980) Behaviour of the red kangaroo, *Macropus rufus* (Desmarest

1822), in northwestern New South Wales, Australia *Australian Mammalogy* 4: 5–58

___ (1981) Social behaviour of the euro, *Macropus robustus* (Gould), in the Australian arid zone *Australian Wildlife Research* 8: 13–49

___ (1987) Socio-ethology of the antilopine wallaroo, *Macropus antilopinus*, in the Northern Territory, with observations on sympatric *M. robustus woodwardi* and *M. agilis*. *Australian Wildlife Research* 14: 243–55

___ (1991) Home range of the red kangaroo *Macropus rufus*. *J. Arid Environments* 20: 83–98

___ (1991) Home range of the euro, *Macropus robustus erubescens*. *J. Arid Environments* 20: 99–111

Jaremovic, R.V. (1984) *Space and time related behaviour in eastern grey kangaroos (Macropus giganteus, Shaw)* PhD thesis, University of New South Wales: Kensington

___ and Croft, D.B. (1991) Social organization of the eastern grey kangaroo (Macropodidae, Marsupialia) in southeastern New South Wales: 1. Groups and group home ranges *Mammalia* 55: 169–85

Jarman, P.J. and Coulson, G. (1989) Dynamics and adaptiveness of grouping in macropods. In *Kangaroos, Wallabies and Rat-kangaroos* (eds Grigg, G., Jarman, P. and Hume, I.) Surrey Beatty & Sons: Chipping Norton, NSW

Oliver, A.J. (1986) *Social organisation and dispersal in the red kangaroo* PhD thesis, Murdoch University: Perth

Priddel, D. (1987) The mobility and habitat utilization of kangaroos. In *Kangaroos: Their Ecology and Management in the Sheep Rangelands of Australia* (eds Caughley, G., Shepherd, N.C. and Short, J.) Cambridge University Press: Cambridge

Taylor, R.J. (1982) Group size in the eastern grey kangaroo, *Macropus giganteus*, and the wallaroo, *Macropus robustus*. *Australian Wildlife Research* 9: 229–37

## CHAPTER 4

Arnold, G.W., Grassia, A., Steven, D.E. and Weeldenburg, J.R. (1991) Population ecology of western grey kangaroos in a remnant of wandoo woodland at Bakers Hill, southern Western *Australia Wildlife Research*, 18: 561–75

Clancy, T.F. (1989). *Factors influencing movement patterns of the euro (Macropus robustus erubescens) in the arid zone* PhD thesis, University of New South Wales: Kensington

Corbertt, L.K. and Newsome, A.E. (1987) The feeding ecology of the dingo: III. Dietary relationships with widely fluctuating prey populations in arid Australia: an hypothesis of alternation of predation *Oecologia* 74: 215–27

Croft, D.B. (1991) Home range of the red kangaroo *Macropus rufus*. *J. Arid Environments* 20: 83–98

Edwards, G.P. (1990) *Competition between red kangaroos and sheep in arid New South Wales* PhD thesis, University of New South Wales: Kensington

Edwards, G.P., Croft, D.B. and Dawson, T.J. (1994) Observations of differential sex/age class mobility in red kangaroos (*Macropus rufus*). *J. Arid Environments*, 27: 169–177

Newsome, A.E. (1977) Imbalance in the sex ratio and age structure of the red kangaroo, *Macropus rufus*, in central Australia. In *The Biology of Marsupials* (eds Stonehouse, B. and Gilmore, D.) Macmillan Press: London

Oliver, A.J. (1986). *Social organization and dispersal in the red kangaroo* PhD thesis, Murdoch University: Perth

Robertshaw, J.D. and Harden, R.H. (1989) Predation on Macropodoidea: a review. In *Kangaroos, Wallabies and Rat-kangaroos* (eds Grigg, G., Jarman, P. and Hume, I.) Surrey Beatty & Sons: Chipping Norton, NSW

Russell, E.M. and Richardson, B.J. (1971) Some observations on the breeding, age structure, dispersion and habitat of populations of *Macropus robustus* and *Macropus antilopinus* (Marsupialia) *J. Zoology*, London 165: 131–42

Speare, R., Donovan, J.A., Thomas, A.D. and Speare, P.J. (1989) Diseases of free-ranging Macropodoidea. In *Kangaroos, Wallabies and Rat-kangaroos* (eds Grigg, G., Jarman, P. and Hume, I.) Surrey Beatty & Sons: Chipping Norton, NSW

Thompson, P. (1992) The behavioural ecology of dingoes in north-western Australia. III. Hunting and feeding behaviour, and diet *Wildlife Research* 19: 531–41

## CHAPTER 5

Croft, D.B. (1981a) Social behaviour of the euro, *Macropus robustus* (Gould), in the Australian arid zone *Australian Wildlife Research* 8: 13–49

____ (1981b) Behaviour of the red kangaroo, *Macropus rufus* (Desmarest 1822), in northwestern New South Wales, Australia *Australian Mammalogy* 4: 5–58

Dawson, T.J. (1983) *Monotremes and Marsupials: The Other Mammals* Edward Arnold: London

Gemmell, R.T. and Rose, R.W. (1989) The senses involved in movement of some newborn Macropodoidea and other marsupials from the cloaca to pouch. In *Kangaroos, Wallabies and Rat-kangaroos* (eds Grigg, G., Jarman, P. and Hume, I.) Surrey Beatty & Sons: Chipping Norton, NSW

Hume, I.D., Jarman, P.J., Renfree, M.B. and Temple-Smith, P.D. (1989) Macropodidae. In *Fauna of Australia*, Volume 1B, Mammalia (eds Walton, D.W. and Richardson, B.J.) Australian Government Publishing Service: Canberra

Jaremovic, R.V. (1984) *Space and time related behaviour in eastern grey kangaroos (Macropus giganteus, Shaw)* PhD thesis, University of New South Wales: Kensington

Jones, R.C. (1989) Reproduction in male Macropodidae. In *Kangaroos, Wallabies and Rat-kangaroos* (eds Grigg, G., Jarman, P. and Hume, I.) Surrey Beatty & Sons: Chipping Norton, NSW

Renfree, M.B., Fletcher, T.P., Blanden, D.R., Lewis, P.R., Shaw, G., Gordon, K., Short, R.V., Parer-Cook, E. and Parer, D. (1989) Physiological and behavioural events around the time of birth in macropodid marsupials. In *Kangaroos, Wallabies and Rat-kangaroos* (eds Grigg, G., Jarman, P. and Hume, I.) Surrey Beatty & Sons: Chipping Norton, NSW

Tyndale-Biscoe, H. (1989) The adaptiveness of reproductive processes. In *Kangaroos,*

*Wallabies and Rat-kangaroos* (eds Grigg, G., Jarman, P. and Hume, I.) Surrey Beatty & Sons: Chipping Norton, NSW

Tyndale-Biscoe, H. and Renfree, M. (1987) *Reproductive Physiology of Marsupials* Cambridge University Press: Cambridge

## CHAPTER 6

Arnold, G.W., Grassia, A., Steven, D.E. and Weeldenburg, J.R. (1991) Population ecology of western grey kangaroos in a remnant of wandoo woodland at Bakers Hill, southern Western Australia *Wildlife Research* 18: 561–75

Clancy, T.F. (1989) *Factors influencing movement patterns of the euro (Macropus robustus erubescens) in the arid zone* Ph D thesis, University of New South Wales: Kensington

Croft, D.B. (1981a) Social behaviour of the euro, *Macropus robustus* (Gould), in the Australian arid zone *Australian Wildlife Research* 8: 13–49

—— (1981b) Behaviour of the red kangaroo, *Macropus rufus* (Desmarest 1822), in northwestern New South Wales, Australia *Australian Mammalogy* 4: 5–58

—— (1987) Socio-ecology of the antilopine wallaroo, *Macropus antilopinus*, in the Northern Territory, with observations on sympatric *M. robustus woodwardi* and *M. agilis. Australian Wildlife Research* 14: 243–55

Ealey, E.H.M. (1967) Ecology of the euro, *Macropus robustus* (Gould), in north-western Australia: IV. Age and growth *CSIRO Wildlife Research* 12: 67–80

Frith, H.J. and Sharman, G.B. (1964) Breeding in wild populations of the red kangaroo, *Megaleia rufa. CSIRO Wildlife Research* 9: 86–114

Merchant, J.C. (1989) Lactation in macropodoid marsupials. In *Kangaroos, Wallabies and Rat-kangaroos* (eds Grigg, G., Jarman, P. and Hume, I.) Surrey Beatty & Sons: Chipping Norton, NSW

Poole, W.E. (1975) Reproduction in the two species of grey kangaroos, *Macropus giganteus* (Shaw) and *M. fuliginosus* (Desmarest): II. Gestation, parturition and pouch life *Australian J. Zoology* 23: 333–53

Poole, W.E. and Catling, P.C. (1974) Reproduction in the two species of grey kangaroos, *Macropus giganteus* Shaw and *M. fuliginosus* (Desmarest). I. Sexual maturity and oestrus *Australian J. Zoology* 22: 277–302

Poole, W.E. and Merchant, J.C. (1987) Reproduction in captive wallaroos: the eastern wallaroo, *Macropus robustus robustus*, the euro, *M. r. erubescens* and the antilopine wallaroo, *M. antilopinus. Australian Wildlife Research* 14: 225–45

Russell, E.M. (1970) Observations on the behaviour of the red kangaroo (*Megaleia rufa*) in captivity *Zeitschrift fur Tierpsychologie* 27: 385–404

—— (1973) Mother–young relations and early behavioural development in the marsupials *Macropus eugenii* and *Megaleia rufa. Zeitschrift fur Tierpsychologie* 33: 163–203

Sharman, G.B. and Calaby, J.H. (1964) Reproductive behaviour in the red kangaroo, *Megaleia rufa*, in captivity *CSIRO Wildlife Research* 9: 58–85

Sharman, G.B., Frith, H.J. and Calaby, J.H. (1964) Growth of the pouch young, tooth eruption and age determination in the red kangaroo, *Megaleia rufa. CSIRO Wildlife Research* 9: 20–49

Shepherd, N. (1987) Condition and recruitment of kangaroos. In *Kangaroos: Their Ecology and Management in the Sheep Rangelands of Australia* (eds Caughley, G., Shepherd, N.C. and Short, J.) Cambridge University Press: Cambridge

Stuart-Dick, R.I. (1987) *Parental investment and rearing schedules in the eastern grey kangaroo* PhD thesis, University of New England: Armidale, NSW

Tyndale-Biscoe, H. and Renfree, M. (1987) *Reproductive Physiology of Marsupials* Cambridge University Press: Cambridge

## CHAPTER 7

Barker, R.D. (1987) The diet of herbivores in sheep rangelands. In *Kangaroos: Their Ecology and Management in the Sheep Rangelands of Australia* (eds Caughley, G., Shepherd, N.C. and Short, J.) Cambridge University Press: Cambridge

Dawson, T.J. (1989) Diets of macropodoid marsupials: general patterns and environmental influences. In *Kangaroos, Wallabies and Rat-kangaroos* (eds Grigg, G., Jarman, P. and Hume, I.) Surrey Beatty & Sons: Chipping Norton, NSW

Dawson, T.J. and Ellis, B. A. (1994) Diets of mammalian herbivores in Australian arid shrublands: seasonal effects on overlap between red kangaroos, sheep and rabbits and on dietary niche breadths and electivities *J. Arid Environments* 26: 257–71

Dellow, D.W. and Hume, I.D. (1982) Studies on the nutrition of macropodine marsupials: IV. Digestion in the stomach and intestine of *Macropus giganteus*, *Thylogale thetis* and *Macropus eugenii. Australian J. Zoology* 30: 767–77

Dudzinski, M.L., Lowe, W.A., Muller, W.J. and Lowe, B.S. (1982) Joint use of habitat by red kangaroos and shorthorn cattle in arid central Australia *Australian J. Ecology* 7: 69–74

Edwards, G.P. (1990) *Competition between red kangaroos and sheep in arid New South Wales* PhD thesis, University of New South Wales: Kensington

Freudenberger, D.O., Wallis, I.R. and Hume, I.D. (1989) Digestive adaptations of kangaroos, wallabies and rat-kangaroos. In *Kangaroos, Wallabies and Rat-kangaroos* (eds Grigg, G., Jarman, P. and Hume, I.) Surrey Beatty & Sons: Chipping Norton, NSW

Hume, I.D. (1982) *Digestive Physiology and Nutrition of Marsupials* Cambridge University Press: Cambridge

Kirkpatrick, T.H. (1965) Studies on the macropodidae in Queensland. 2. Age estimation in the grey kangaroo, the red kangaroo, the eastern wallaroo and the red-necked wallaby, with notes on dental abnormalities *Queensland J. Agricultural and Animal Sciences* 22: 301–17

Sanson, G.D. (1989) Morphological adaptations of teeth to diets and feeding in the Macropodoidea. In *Kangaroos, Wallabies and Rat-kangaroos* (eds Grigg, G., Jarman, P. and Hume, I.) Surrey Beatty & Sons: Chipping Norton, NSW

Stevens, C.E. (1988) *Comparative Physiology of the Vertebrate Digestive System* Cambridge University Press: Cambridge

## CHAPTER 8

Dawson, T.J. (1983) *Monotremes and Marsupials: The Other Mammals* Edward Arnold: London

____ (1989) Responses to cold of monotremes and marsupials *Advances in Comparative and Environmental Physiology* 4: 255–88

Dawson, T.J. and Denny, M.J.S. (1969) A bioclimatological comparison of the summer day microenvironments of two species of arid zone kangaroo *Ecology* 50: 328–32

Dawson, T.J., Denny, M.J.S., Russell, E.M. and Ellis, B.A. (1975) Water use and diet preferences of free ranging kangaroos, sheep and feral goats *J. Zoology, London* 177: 1–23

Dawson, T.J., Robertshaw, D. and Taylor, C.R. (1974) Sweating in the kangaroo: a cooling mechanism during exercise, but not in the heat *American J. Physiology* 227: 494–8

Denny, M.J.S. (1973) *Water relations in arid zone macropodids* PhD thesis, University of New South Wales: Kensington

Freudenberger, D.O. and Hume, I.D. (1992) Ingestive and digestive responses to dietary fibre and nitrogen by two macropodid marsupials (*Macropus robustus erubescens* and *M. r. robustus*) and a ruminant (*Capra hircus*). *Australian J. Zoology* 40: 181–94

McCarron, H.C.K. (1990) *Environmental physiology of the eastern grey kangaroo* (*Macropus giganteus,* Shaw) PhD thesis, University of New South Wales: Kensington

McCarron, H.C.K. and Dawson, T.J. (1989) Thermal relations of Macropodoidea in hot environments. In *Kangaroos, Wallabies and Rat-kangaroos* (eds Grigg, G., Jarman, P. and Hume, I.) Surrey Beatty & Sons: Chipping Norton, NSW

## CHAPTER 9

Croft, D.B. (1992) The relationship between people and animals: an Australian perspective. In *Australian People and Animals in Today's Dreamtime: The Role of Comparative Psychology in the Management of Natural Resources* (ed. Croft, D.B.) Praeger: New York

Finlayson, H.H. (1943) *The Red Centre: Man and Beast in the Heart of Australia* Angus & Robertson: Sydney

Frakes, L.A., McGowran, B. and Bowler, J.M. (1987) Evolution of Australian environments. In *Fauna of Australia*, Volume 1A, General Articles (eds Dyne, G.R. and Walton, D.W.) Australian Government Publishing Service: Canberra

Murray, P. (1991) The Pleistocene megafauna. In *Vertebrate Palaeontology of Australasia* (eds Vickers-Rich, P., Monaghan, J.M., Baird, R.F. and Rich, T.H.) Monash University Publications Committee: Melbourne

Tunbridge, D. (1988) *Flinders Ranges Dreaming* Aboriginal Studies Press: Canberra

____ (1991) *The Story of the Flinders Ranges Mammals* Kangaroo Press: Kenthurst, NSW

## CHAPTER 10

Caughley, G., Shepherd, N.C. and Short, J. eds (1987) *Kangaroos: their Ecology and Management in the Sheep Rangelands of Australia* Cambridge University Press: Cambridge

Denny, M.J.S. (1980) *Red Kangaroo Arid Zone Studies* Unpublished report to Australian National Parks and Wildlife Service; cited with permission

Finney, C.M. (1894) *To Sail Beyond the Sunset: Natural History in Australia 1699–1829* Rigby Publishers: Sydney

Gibson, L.M. and Young, M.D. (1988) *Kangaroos: Counting the Cost* Project Report No. 4, CSIRO Division of Wildlife and Rangelands Research: Deniliquin, NSW

Gould, J. (1973) *Kangaroos* Doubleday & Co: New York (First published in 1863 as Volume II of *The Mammals of Australia*; Modern commentaries by J.M. Dixon).

Lavery, H.J. ed. (1985) *The Kangaroo Keepers* University of Queensland Press: St Lucia

Lunney, D. and Grigg, G. eds (1988) Kangaroo harvesting and the conservation of arid and semi-arid lands *Australian Zoologist* 23: no. 3

Shepherd, N.C. (1983) The feasibility of farming kangaroos *Australian Rangelands Journal* 5: 35–44

Rudd, S. (1953) *On Our Selection* and *Our New Selection*. Angus & Robertson: Sydney (Australian Literary Heritage Series); first published 1899 and 1903, Bulletin Newspaper Co: Sydney

# INDEX